HAUNTED
NOTTINGHAM

HAUNTED
NOTTINGHAM

ANDREW JAMES WRIGHT

TEMPUS

Frontispiece: *This strange effect was captured in one of the many allegedly haunted caverns below the streets.*

First published 2006
Reprinted 2007

Tempus Publishing Limited
The Mill, Brimscombe Port,
Stroud, Gloucestershire, GL5 2QG
www.tempus-publishing.com

© Andrew James Wright 2006

The right of Andrew James Wright to be identified as the Author
of this work has been asserted in accordance with the
Copyrights, Designs and Patents Act 1988.

British Library Cataloguing in Publication Data.
A catalogue record for this book is available from the British Library.

ISBN 978 0 7524 4194 8

Typesetting and origination by Tempus Publishing Limited.
Printed in Great Britain.

CONTENTS

ABOUT THE AUTHOR

Andrew James Wright was born in Leicester in 1955. He has been involved in the music business, running a pub and now works at the University of Leicester. A ghost investigator for thirty years (although he admits to having never seen a ghost), his other interests include: pubs, gardening, fishing, ferrets and swimming.

ACKNOWLEDGEMENTS

Dr Alan Gauld. Samantha Marriott and UK Paranormal for giving me access to their reports. Trevor Dickson at The NCCL Galleries of Justice (the bravest man in Nottingham for spending night after night in the building!). Brian Rigby at The Bell Inn. Kim at The White Hart. The staff of Ye Olde Trip to Jerusalem, especially Claire, Jodie and Stuart, and The Nottingham Historical and Archaeological Society (especially Michael).

A special mention of thanks must be extended to Nottingham ghost researcher Louise Marriott. She did much of the photography and searched out vintage prints for inclusion. As well as conducting vital research, Louise also wrote the last chapter and so should receive recognition for this valuable input.

I compiled this selection using an antique map of Nottingham, and I ask the reader's forgiveness if one or two stories would be better suited to another section of the book. I hope that you enjoy reading *Haunted Nottingham*.

FOREWORD

Nottingham began in the sixth century as a small Saxon settlement called 'Snotta ing ham'. In the late ninth century the Danes turned Nottingham into a fortified settlement; the town had a ditch dug around it and an earth rampart with a wooden palisade on top, like a hill fort. William the Conqueror built a timber castle to guard the town in 1067. Nottingham had a population of around 1,000 at the time of the Norman Conquest. In 1155 the King gave the town a charter, a document granting the townsfolk certain rights. In 1449 the town gained its first sheriff.

The population of Nottingham was 5,000 in the late seventeenth century. In the early eighteenth century Daniel Defoe, author of *Robinson Crusoe*, enthusiastically described Nottingham as 'one of the most pleasant and beautiful towns in England'. The wool, stoneware and lace industry flourished and by the standards of the time, Nottingham became an important town.

In the nineteenth century Nottingham gained gas street lighting, piped water, its first proper police force, a prison and a university college. Parks were created and the now famous Goose Fair moved from the market square to Forest Park. According to legend the fair came about in 1290 after an angler on the River Trent landed a huge pike: he lifted his rod high in the air and a passing goose took the pike, the rod and the angler! It dropped the angler in the market square and as he survived unharmed a public holiday was announced: it lasted twenty-one days

In 1952 a statue of Robin Hood was erected by the castle. The Playhouse theatre opened in 1963. The Broad Marsh shopping centre was built in 1972 with the larger Victoria mall opening three years later. By the late twentieth century the main industries in the city were tobacco, textiles, pharmaceuticals, printing and bicycles. And now is a thriving inner city.

Of course Nottingham has its mysteries and legends. Anyone who has wandered at twilight around the quiet streets of the Lace Market, Newstead Abbey or Woolaton Park will realise that it is mysterious, even perhaps unsettling, and only the foolhardy would walk the huge church cemetery at dusk. The castle with its tunnels and the quiet little avenues can play on one's nerves in the night. We know that an atmosphere is created over many years and seeps into the very fabric of a building or area. Sometimes an atmosphere will be compacted, strong enough to send a shiver down one's spine. Some might experience a feeling of being observed, others may glimpse a dark shadow where there should not be one. Nottingham has its ghosts.

Lime Avenue, Wollaton Hall. (courtesy of David Ottewell)

ONE

AROUND THE CITY

Wollaton Hall

Wollaton Hall is a huge, formidable pile standing in over 500 acres of deer park and woodland. It was built by Francis Willoughby and took eight years to complete in 1588. The hall and grounds have long held the tradition of being a most haunted and enchantingly mystical place. There have, of course, been many characters living here over the years, some of whom may still linger spiritually. Sir Hugh Willoughby was an arctic explorer who met a watery end in the mid-1500s whilst attempting to get to India. The famous naturalist Francis Willoughby and noted diarist Cassandra have all left their mark on Wollaton.

Shortly after 1925 the entire estate was auctioned off: the Nottingham Corporation bought it for £200,000. Today Wollaton Hall is used to house exhibits of the Nottingham Natural History Museum and also its industrial past. There are conducted tours of the museum and periodic evening tours by private arrangement: on these one may encounter one of the many phantoms abroad here.

In the early 1980s, two of the museum research staff were chatting to a foreman in a quiet room when their attention was caught by a sound of heavy, laboured breathing, like an asthmatic. They all listened to the peculiar sound and noted it was in the room with them and seemed to be moving around. They looked around in mute astonishment as the sound then moved over to a dark recess where it remained before slowly fading away. It had a very unsettling effect on the three witnesses. During the Christmas break of 1988 one of the security operatives was looking into the Great Hall when he was abruptly tapped on the shoulder. He jolted and turned around but there was no one there! The man was all too aware of the claims of others experiencing the same sensation and simply left it at that.

The long coaching drive, Lime Avenue, was the scene of a truly haunting vision. Even during the day the numerous lime trees that line the avenue create a dark, slightly unsettling gloominess. At night of course this would feel most sinister indeed. It was on a dark night that one of the residents of the several courtyard flats was returning home after visiting friends. It was just after midnight as he passed the golf pavilion when he observed ahead, under the dark veil of the lime trees, two cloaked figures. He stopped still and noted that they appeared to be engaged in

The enigmatic and forbidding Wollaton Hall around the early 1900s.

The huge gatehouse of Wollaton Hall. This still exists and reflects the huge size of the estate.

vigorous conversation but yet were silent. After a short time the young man felt intimidated and felt the figures to be ghosts: he came away hurriedly.

A man in the deer park at dusk was slowly and quietly moving around the woodland glades in order to observe and photograph some of the many foxes and badgers that inhabit the grounds. After creeping up on a fox cub and taking a photograph he decided to pack up as the light began to fail. He then saw a lantern moving fluidly through a large tight thicket. He watched in amazement as the lamp swung from side to side: it was as if the bush did not exist. He packed up and fled the scene.

The Minstrel's Gallery in the hall is reputed to harbour a musical phantom no less! One evening an attendant was engaged in locking up the Main Hall when he heard footsteps emanating from the gallery. Puzzled, the attendant listened, then heard an undistinguishable but audible tune being whistled. The man met a colleague and together they investigated but found no rational explanation at all. Later, as they were locking the front doors, they both heard the footsteps and whistling tune emanate again. Baffled completely, they hastily locked up and got out, leaving the musical ghost alone. Periodically, visitors at a winter's dusk may glimpse a military spectre gliding swiftly around the courtyards.

During the Second World War, Nissen huts were constructed on an area known as the Forty Acre. Barbed wire was put around the compound for good measure as both German and Italian prisoners of war were billeted. In time, some of the higher ranking officers were allowed to mix with the British in the hall and adjacent courtyards. In the late 1980s, a lady observed a uniformed German officer in one of the courtyards; as is so often the case, the figure became less defined before fading away. The observer was just in the right state of mind to behold this psychic image of the past.

Sounds of a phantom so loud and clear that people quickly move out of the way have been experienced on one of the long avenues between Derby Road and Harrow Road. Claimants of this experience describe a steady trot of hoof beats and a snorting sound in close proximity. They then naturally leap aside, only to realise that nothing is there (although the sounds pass and move away). Most unsettling! Even more so must be the atmosphere some of the more receptive souls pick up on when wandering the marshy edges of the two lakes in the parkland, Wollaton Park Lake and Martin's Pond. During the last two World Wars several women committed suicide here after losing their husbands or sons in action. Nothing is seen or heard as one gazes over the deep, silent waters but the sinister essence of the anguish at pacing backwards and forward, trying to get the courage to jump in and drown, has left a depressing gloom of wasted life.

Keith Taylor in his *Ghosts of Wollaton* relates a curious incident he experienced whilst pursuing his passion for photographing deer. It was a crisp December dusk in 1972. He and fellow enthusiast, John Sutton, were in the paddocks, where with the twilight a bank of mist began to descend. After obtaining several rather splendid photographs of red deer the pair made their way towards Middleton's Paddock where they caught sight of an unusually tall man in the distance striding on a hill towards a gate. Even in the poor light they both observed him to be dressed in a wide-brimmed hat, a rough coat, waistcoat and gumboots. He had a short beard with weather-beaten features and held a stick in his left hand. As soon as the man touched the gate, the stags got to their feet and bounded off towards the chestnut grove. The man then waved his stick vigorously in the air before striding away into the darkness.

The event had a lasting impression on Keith so he thought to carry out some research in order to find out who the man was or used to be. He eventually discovered that in the 1920s there were two gamekeepers, Billy Archer and Charlie Edge. Billy was quite slight and did not seem to fit, but Charlie's description seemed very similar to the mysterious figure. Charlie Edge had always carried a short wooden stick with him, and had been gored by a stag during an autumn rutting season. Was this the lone figure who strode into the gloom on that dark December dusk?

Without doubt the most bizarre incident at Wollaton occurred in September 1979. Four children aged between eight and ten claimed to have seen around sixty small people riding in pairs in little red and white vehicles like bubble cars. The beings were around two feet in height, although this was difficult to judge as they were all sitting. Apparently they just appeared from nowhere and kept careering around the swampy ground near the lake. They had yellow tights, blue tops and long caps with bobbles on the end not unlike Victorian nightcaps. They seemed quite jolly and were cackling.

After a minute or two they all vanished, leaving the four astonished children staring in amazement – one girl was so stunned she fell into the mud. It later came about that one girl, Angela, had glimpsed a similar creature a few weeks earlier in some woodland nearby. Were they fairies or gnomes? There is the suggestion by spiritualist mediums that ghosts or psychic influences may show themselves in various guises. Perhaps this was the case here. The children interpreted the vision as mystical beings, and some have suggested that they may have been from another planet! On an amusing note there was a similar tale elsewhere in Britain concerning a woodsman sitting on a log having his lunch. Suddenly a little car appeared with a small man wearing a similar hat. The small open-topped car drew up to the stunned lumberjack: the little man reached out and took one of his cheese sandwiches then drove away giving a V sign!

Olfactory sensations are the commonest forms of psychic influences: the author has experienced them on numerous occasions. Two visitors were strolling towards the park gates on a September dusk. They were near the kitchen gardens when a strong scent filled the air. Both naturalists, they knew it not to be of animal origin: it was more like a musky scent which had been manufactured. Interested, they decided to follow the strange aroma. It took them across Lime Avenue and onto Beeston Lodge where it ended: a mystery indeed! One theory was that they followed a psychic force from the main gates to the lodge where two families once resided.

An unseen ghost is said to idly wander the gardens from time to time. Presumably the ghost is a former gardener or simply admires the blooms on display. In the early 1980s the head gardener heard mysterious footsteps. It was around 11 p.m. as he began hosing the gardens: there was a drought, and it was particularly hot, so late evening was best to water the plants and flowers. He became aware of someone approaching and looked around, but there was no one to be seen. The dazed gardener carried on. The footfalls seemed dainty, like those of a woman. The footfalls moved away so the gardener followed: they followed the south terrace, then past the goldfish pond to the sundial and down the stone steps by the rose garden. A few evenings later the gardener heard them again whilst rolling up the long hose. It was around the same time, 11 p.m. The footsteps passed very close then moved away. The man then got a faint essence of a rich perfume that only lasted for a second or two. There is a similar account by a young boy who climbed over the hedge into the grounds with friends in the mid-1980s. He and the others heard the dainty footsteps and hastily got back over the hedge.

It seems that the majority of the Wollaton ghosts are just heard or sensed but there have been sightings. Lenton Priory once existed on the west side of Wollaton Park, although no evidence remains of the structure. Much of the land is now occupied by lodges, outbuildings, sports grounds and annexes of Nottingham University. One witness claims to have observed five phantom monks walking along the path by the university sports pavilion. More than one resident nearby has been awoken to see a cowled monk in the room who faded away after a few seconds.

As this book was going to press my researcher heard recent news of paranormal activity here. A young chap went to visit his sister, who rents a room in one of the large Victorian buildings that surround the hall. Wanting some peace from the rest of her roommates, he went to her room and lay on the bed.

He had just closed his eyes when he was overcome by a feeling of nausea and the urge to open his eyes again. What he saw would make him wish he hadn't, for floating over him was a bald gentleman looking intently into his face. As one might expect, he closed his eyes again and started yelling for help. When he dared look again the spirit had vanished. Later he was able to give his sister a better description: the figure was a cream colour and totally transparent with no legs.

The Salutation Inn

The Salutation Inn on Maid Marion Way looks much like any other city-centre alehouse. It is only when viewed from the rear that one realises it is quite an ancient building. The date AD 1240 is displayed on the apex wall, which is another clue to its long history. At this time the building was a leather tannery. The workshop was on the ground floor and in the upper reaches, the tannery had living accommodation. There were also rooms for some of the workers, a cottage industry. Two hundred years later it is thought the building was a private residence owned by a Mr John Alastre.

The Salutation; a phantom highwayman fights off his captors here.

In 1649 Cromwell came to power and formed the Commonwealth Government. The Puritans were less than impressed with the inn sign, which depicted the Archangel Gabriel saluting the Virgin Mary. They ordered the landlord to take the thing down or to repaint the sign. The landlord was stuck for an idea for another depiction of the pub name for the huge timber sign. Eventually he decided to rename the pub: he called it, 'The Soldier and Citizen.' Eleven years later, in 1660, the landlord changed the pub name and sign back to The Salutation Inn as the monarchy had been restored. The new sign depicted a handshake.

The pub has seen a long line of licensees and the usual drama of pub life throughout the seventeenth and eighteenth centuries. Beneath the pub there is a network of tunnels and caves. In 1937 an investigation by the Thoroton Excavation Society concluded that the ancient caves may date from the ninth century and that Saxons would have lived in them. A ghost of little more than a toddler is alleged to dolefully wander these dank and shadowy caves. A girl child of possible two or three years old has been glimpsed silently drifting in and out of the shadows.

I spent a night in the tunnels and caves in June 2003. A Greek colleague, Paula Christodoulou, arranged a study of the site and invited me along. I came over with American ghost hunter Linda Tweed and met up with Nottingham historian Robert Waldram in the bustling market square. It was a Friday evening and the town is renowned for its nightlife: a party of drunken 'hens' with the intended bride adorned with little more than an L plate made a cheery comment about my fancy shirt! We arrived just before midnight after strolling by the castle. It was quite a muggy night so it felt quite pleasant below ground. The scenario was not unlike a horror film set: dark, winding tunnels and huge caverns. Paula had set up an ultraviolet lamp to enhance any weird visual effects that occurred.

In the late 1990s a ghost became active for a while, performing the usual types of pointless mischief. One landlord had the pub keys vanish from behind the bar late one evening. Baffled, he went upstairs in case he might have somehow mislaid them but his search was fruitless. Totally perplexed, he went back downstairs and found them swinging on the hook behind the bar! His wife had an experience of some kind of intense force field in the cellar and was so unsettled by it she refused ever to go down there again.

There are assumed to be two other phantoms in the building, one a former landlord who got into a state of depression and committed suicide by poisoning himself. He is apparently to be seen moving erratically about the pub. The other spectre is undoubtedly a 'replay', as they are known. A replay-type apparition is where a particular event is somehow retained into the fabric of a place and replays itself like a film. Captured in time, the apparition is totally unaware of the present and is firmly in its own period of time. Here there is a highwayman who is seen sitting down: he then leaps up and pulls out a pair of flintlock pistols and shouts mutely at an unseen assailant. The pistols are then fired and the phantom vanishes. In 1730 a highwayman was arrested here so it is assumed this incident is the replay.

Our night was uneventful with no ghosts seen or heard, but that is so often the case when one goes in search of these aloof phantoms.

The old Hippo Club

One would imagine that the last place for a mournful wraith to linger would be a noisy discotheque, hardly the ideal conditions for a silent ghost to exist: they tend to prefer tranquil places.

The entrance to the old Hippo Club on Bridlesmith Gate.

Of course, it is the history of a site, not what use it may be converted to over the years, that hold the clues to who might haunt. Centuries ago, Bridlesmith Gate was part of the early Saxon settlement and the premises noted here sat on the edge of the weekday market. One of the few remaining old buildings on busy Bridlesmith Gate, The Hippo Club had a series of sporadic happenings during some structural alterations in 1969.

Weird cold areas, loud bumps and bangs, and a sensation of being watched were reported by contractors during the work. The most frightening event during the unrest occurred after a basement room was discovered. The manager felt compelled to visit the little room one evening. He entered and stood trembling at the scene. There was a table with a figure sitting at it on a wooden chair. The figure was dressed as a Quaker, but had no face: just an oval white mist.

Paranormal events didn't end there. The Nottingham Historical & Archaeological Society has spent many hours excavating and mapping the thousands of caves that lie below the city. It is thanks to their hard work that so much of Nottingham's history has been saved from destruction. Some eight years ago they started tracking the series of caves lying under Bridlesmith Gate. Starting under the Oxfam Shop they extend under Bridlesmith Gate to beneath the row of shops opposite. Working their way along, after some time the archaeologists found themselves outside the Hippo Club, which was in full swing. While they waited for closing time the team chatted to the bouncers, and the conversation turned to ghosts.

Part of the bouncer's duties was the make sure the building was clear of revellers, as there were many little nooks anyone intent on making off with some after-hours beer could hide in until the coast was clear. One of the gentlemen found himself down in the lower cave where he saw what he later described as an older man in a dirty brown outfit moving around. He called to his colleagues above who came down the narrow stairway and fanned out but could find no trace of the intruder. Putting it down to tiredness they thought nothing more of it.

The archaeologists finally got access too and found themselves in a natural cave blocked off at the back by a brick wall into which was set a plastic air outlet. Realising they could not track the cave any further they recorded their findings and left.

Two years later the Nottingham Historical and Archaeological Society were given access to what was then a rubble-strewn block of land on the corner of Bridlesmith Gate and Middle Pavement. According to the old maps they had sourced there should be a well on the land and they finally found it several days later and started to excavate it. Working with them at the time was a young lad doing work experience. As is often the case, he was eager to get involved, but got more then he bargained for when left to sweep up at the end of the dig. Given a broom, he was sent to the area blocked off by a familiar brick wall with a plastic air outlet. Minutes later he came charging out of the hole very pale and shaking. He had not been working for long when his attention was drawn to something behind him. Turning around he watched what he described as an old man, dressed entirely in a rough, brown garment, who floated directly out of the Hippo Club wall and towards him.

Works Nightclub (formally the Evening Post Building)

During the late 1990s the *Nottingham Evening Post* newspaper moved from their old home on Forman Street to a newly built building on Canal Street. The old building was demolished and a leisure complex was built on the land. Now there are restaurants, a cinema, many eateries and a nightclub called The Works there. In 2000 the manager of the nightclub got in touch with EMGIG, a local paranormal group, because he thought the place was haunted. EMGIG assembled a team and invited several members of UK Paranormal and Yorkshire-based medium Jacqueline Adair to investigate the building.

It situated at the back of the leisure complex, and surprisingly large, with rooms upstairs disguising a vast open space below ground. It was in this area that the medium, Jacqui, picked up on a very persistent spirit who led them a merry dance through the cavernous room until they found themselves in the toilets, where she was puzzled by the message that there was something on the other side of the wall that would explain who the spook was.

It was only when they were joined by the manager again that he pointed out a side corridor running along the inside edge of the toilet block that was no wider than a service area. A metal ladder was bolted to the wall. The medium felt a strong urge to climb the ladder as soon as she saw it: it was found to lead to a small, empty room. Whilst she was looking at it she got the impression that the entity had 'lived' in that alcove but this made even less sense to us.

The spirit refused to identify himself but did give some impressions of his working life, but much to Jacqui's frustration she had to leave without getting a name. She did, however, confirm that the little tricks being played on the staff were down to the elusive spook and that it meant no harm. A message was passed on to the manager that the spirit had especially taken to him, seeing in him the same hard-working ambition that the spirit had been known for in life.

With these few clues to his character Jacqui set off back to her home in Yorkshire and the team took their scant details back to the *Nottingham Evening Post*. At first they drew a blank. Many of the older staff had retired and many of the newer folk hadn't even worked in the old building, but such is the interest in the paranormal that word got around and a couple of weeks later word reached the team about a gentleman who fitted the bill.

His name has been lost in time, but even now he is remembered for his hard work, moonlighting as a journalist and spending many a day (and night) at the back of the building in its vast paper store. This was in the day of the old printing presses and he often found himself working through the night to help get the early edition ready. And it was at these times that he slept in a small alcove he had found and kitted out with a small bed, reached by a ladder bolted to the wall.

Nottingham Castle

The first thing the train traveller arriving in Nottingham is likely to see is the castle, perched 130ft above the town. It bears little resemblance to a castle nowadays but nevertheless that is what it is. The first Norman castle was a timber structure of a motte and bailey design, built in 1067, one year after the Battle of Hastings, by order of William the Conqueror. A few years later this was replaced by an imposing stone structure.

For centuries the castle served as one of the most important fortifications for royalty and nobles alike with its position in the centre of the British Isles. It was also a popular place for leisure activities such as hunting in the nearby royal forests of Barnsdale and Sherwood. Whilst the King of England, Richard the Lionheart, was away at the Third Crusade (with a vast number of English noblemen), it was claimed that the castle was occupied by the Sheriff of Nottingham. Of course this may be a flight of fancy, as in the legends of Robin Hood; the castle was the scene of many skirmishes in the popular stories.

In 1194, a historical battle took place at the castle when the supporters of Prince John captured it. The fortification was the scene of a decisive siege when King Richard I returned to England and besieged the castle; he was aided by David of Scotland and Ranulph de Blouderville, the 4th Earl of Chester.

Nottingham Castle would see many changes over the following centuries until it became obsolete in the sixteenth century. During the Civil War the site was the scene of several bloody skirmishes which added to the deterioration of the once proud castle. Towards the end of the Civil War, Charles I chose Nottingham as the rallying point for his armies, but shortly after his departure the castle rock was made defensible and held by the Parliamentarians. Commanded by Colonel John Hutchinson, they fended off several Royalist attacks. They were the last group to hold the castle. After the execution of Charles I in 1649 the castle was totally razed to the ground.

The present structure was built after the restoration of Charles II in 1660 by Henry Cavendish, the 2nd Duke of Newcastle, as a castle mansion house. It lost its attraction to the later dukes with the arrival of the Industrial Revolution.

Nottingham gained the reputation of having the worst slums in the British Empire. During violent rioting in 1831 by those living in slum conditions the mansion was set alight. The mansion remained as a derelict shell until 1878 as a sorry reminder of the state of affairs and those responsible for it. Eventually it was restored as the Nottingham Castle Museum and opened by King Edward VII. It is without doubt an enduring symbol of the city and a popular place for both local inhabitants and tourists to visit. Fine views can be obtained as a reward for the tiring trek to the motte summit.

Nottingham Castle. The old fortification has seen many changes over the years. This view shows just how difficult it would be to attack it.

In the sixteenth century the castle bore no resemblance to what exists today.

THE CASTLE, NOTTINGHAM.

In Victorian times a tree-lined avenue led to the castle.

Another later change to the castle was the addition of a rather grand gateway.

Queen Isabella, a formidable character whose pleas were heard long after her demise.

The defences of the castle and the task involved in attempting to attack it were significant. 'To attack the castle is an awesome task and you can only admire King Richard's valiant, almost reckless attempt to storm it. Since the south and west cliffs are 130 feet high, the defenders only have to defend the north and east and if you look closely at the castle's fortifications on these sides you will find that the walls are very strong'.

Under the castle, carved into the sandstone outcrop on which the structure rests, is a well-known tunnel called 'Mortimer's Hole'. I went down there by appointment in 1987 one afternoon and found it to be most eerie, to say the least. It is easy to let one's mind conjure up unpleasant scenes in such a dark, dank place. Sir Roger Mortimer, the Earl of March, was thought to have murdered Edward II on the night of 19 October 1330. He was having an affair with Queen Isabella and they were both in the castle. Edward's son, the young King Edward III, entered the network of secret tunnels that ultimately led into the castle itself. With a band of loyal supporters, the King burst into his mother's bed chamber and found the Queen and Mortimer. Edward seized Sir Roger Mortimer and the band led him away. The Queen cried out in vain, 'Fair son, have pity on the gentle Mortimer'.

He was imprisoned in the castle keep and then transferred to the Tower of London, where he was later subjected to the barbaric treatment of being hung, drawn and quartered. The tunnel that led to his eventual downfall became locally known as Mortimer's Hole. No wonder then that an unearthly presence sometimes makes itself known to unsuspecting tourists whilst on guided tours. The guide will have told the story and thoughts will be directed towards the wretched Mortimer.

Of course there has been mental turmoil, suffering and violent death in and around the castle which may have left an indelible stain on the fabric of the place. Some of the ghosts who are said to linger here are thought to be noble, even royal: King Henry II, King John, Queen Isabella. The poor wretches left to rot in the dungeons may also linger in mournful spirit.

In 1212, King John held some twenty-eight sons of Welsh noble families hostage in the castle. The boys, some quite young, lived in the castle for quite a long period and were treated reasonably. Then one day King John ordered that all the hostages were to be executed. The boys' terrified screams rang around the echoing walls of the castle as one after the other was dragged to the ramparts and hanged. It is claimed that their shrill screams and pleas for mercy are still heard in the castle precincts.

In the early 1990s, in one of the galleries, the Bonnington Room, a burglar alarm was activated in the middle of the night. The in-house security guards waited for the police to be dispatched to the castle before entering. On their arrival, the party entered the castle; a police dog was brought in for good measure. They patrolled the dark and silent museum with nothing found to be amiss. On entering the Bonnington Room the lights all came on although no one was near the switches. The dog then became unsettled and behaved unusually for a trained animal. It began to whine and cowered with its tail tucked under and its hackles up; the dog was indeed distressed. Over the years the story has been embellished somewhat and it has been told that the dog was found next morning and that its hair had turned white!

There is a legend that if one is alone in the Long Gallery one would be prudent to admire the fine art and nothing else as it is said that the ghost of the Countess of Nottingham sometimes appears to those alone. According to the legend, if you glimpse the phantom you will be dead within the year. Perhaps the most enduring phantom is that of Queen Isabella. She is said to have joined an order of nuns in an effort to cleanse her soul but she instead went insane and was eventually incarcerated within Castle Rising's keep in north Norfolk. Awful screams emanating from the bleak and windswept keep in the night are thought to be her mad outbursts, which have terrified those unwise enough to go near the place.

Can a ghost haunt more than one location? In theory, the answer is yes. Strong emotional impressions may indeed be absorbed into the very fabric as an atmosphere that will then build up and eventually release itself on some unfortunate. Let us also dwell on the theory that old stone harbours the elements from which recording devices and microchips are made. It is known as 'the stone tape theory'; the very stone is acting as a recording machine. Isabella may indeed linger within Nottingham Castle and wander in morose torment and remorse.

Perhaps the most authenticated and well-known account comes from a dark night during the Second World War. Ye Olde Trip to Jerusalem was a popular watering hole for many of the 'Yanks' whilst stationed at the many USAAF (United States Army Air Force) bases around Nottinghamshire and Lincolnshire. Late one night a group of 'GIs' left the pub during a period of blackout: they had 'had a few' and there was much jollity and shouting as they walked up the hill. Then, above their cheerful chatting, a shrill, bloodcurdling scream filled the air: then a loud female voice was heard. The sentence she shouted was described as being in a 'foreign lingo' and stopped them all in their tracks. They saw nothing anywhere but the sound seemed to come from up at the dark castle. It shook them all.

Perhaps the piteous pleas they heard were, 'Bel fitz, eiez pitie du gentil Mortimer'. Queen Isabella was French, and as we recall when King Edward dragged Mortimer, away her response as recorded by history was, 'Fair son have pity on the gentle Mortimer'.

Trent Bridge

Perhaps the most popular, method, if that is the right word, for those wishing to rid themselves of this cruel world is committing suicide either by jumping from a good height or drowning. Anyone who might have swallowed water in a swimming pool or simply choked on a drink will know how horrendous the experience is. Those scared of heights such as the present author will be aware of the anxiety they can cause. To make certain, I suppose, jumping from a great height into deep water ensures that if one does not kill you the other will.

Trent Bridge, a well-known landmark that has its gloomy side.

Dark figures have been reported at night on Trent Bridge that leap into the river without leaving a ripple and the sensitive may feel a chill up the spine and sense the presence of ghostly people pacing about before leaping into the cold, dark river.

Canal Street

In 1976 there was a supposed set of ghostly disturbances at a former police station and mortuary on Canal Street in the city. At the time a firm producing fireplaces occupied the premises.

Strange sounds were reported by those arriving first in the morning. A light was also found to be on in the corridor although it was turned off by those leaving in the evening, and one nervous lady complained of dreadful moaning sounds.

When the claims got out to the media several 'psychics' offered to 'cleanse' the building: one explained that a strong presence haunted a former cell near where the light kept coming on. The boss, Roy Parsons, was having none of it and decided to investigate himself. He arrived early one morning and let himself in. Sure enough, the light was on. He knew a thing or two about electronics and established that the fluorescent tube was faulty and would flash off so that people leaving would assume it was switched off. On turning the other lights on he listened as the starter began to bang before the light fully kicked in. This would explain the banging: case closed.

When the building was a police station and mortuary a body was brought in. The unfortunate 'corpse' was in fact a person in a catatonic state. The person recovered enough to stagger from the mortuary into the police station before collapsing. An ambulance was called and dispatched but the person died. Although rational explanations were found for the light and the banging, the dreadful groans were never satisfactorily explained.

Church (Rock) Cemetery

Church Cemetery is 150 years old and was founded in 1856 by Edwin Patchitt for the Church Cemetery Company. It covers some thirteen acres and lies north of the town on Mansfield Road and Forest Road East. It was laid on old sandpits and slopes northwards, forming a natural hollow known locally as St Anne's Valley. There were once three windmills and one of the adjacent little cottages was used as a temporary chapel until the mortuary chapel was built in 1879; this was demolished in 1965.

The class system is well in evidence here with elaborate Edwardian and Victorian sculptured tombs and huge monuments in contrast to the paupers' graves where entire families were interred in one large grave. A lodge just within the main gate stands on the site of the gallows and if you take a walk through the area you will easily find the remains of Nottingham's bear pit, a rough-hewn corridor still showing signs of rooms where the terrified animals might have been held.

Also locally known as Rock Cemetery, the place is a haven for wildlife with rabbits, squirrels, foxes and all manner of birds, a pleasant spot to wander aimlessly about or sit and contemplate, strangely silent at times and a million miles away from the busy Mansfield Road.

Church cemetery, a winding place with a ghost or two.

The old lodge where the gallows once stood.

In the late 1960s, a monumental sculptor by the name of Roger Smeeton was laboriously chiselling in an inscription on a memorial stone when his concentration was disturbed by an unsettling sensation: he felt his scalp prickle then 'goosebumps' began to form. He looked around and froze; just a few feet away stood a woman dressed in Victorian period dress. Mr Smeeton thought it odd that he had not heard her approach on the gravel path. Puzzled, Roger turned back to the stone then felt compelled to look at the woman again but she was not there anymore. He stood up and looked around but he was alone: she had simply vanished.

Over by where one of the windmills used to stand is a very secluded part of the cemetery. There have been occasional sightings of an old lady who forms, stands and stares at the beholder before slowly fading away.

North Wilford Power Station

Considering ghosts have an affinity with electricity and are thought to be composed of electrons and neutrons it is not surprising that power stations and areas around sub-stations harbour psychic influences.

The power station on Wilford Road has now been pulled down but a ghost called 'Old George' used to haunt part of the huge station. He was a small man with a check shirt, blue bib and brace overalls and a flat cloth cap. In 1967, during a night shift, Sam Pykett had just shut down the pumps in the Screen Room, where the water from the river is filtered and pumped through in order to cool the turbines. He began the unsavoury task of clearing leaves and other debris away from the screens. Sam suddenly noticed an inexplicable change in the atmosphere: then the air temperature seemed to drop considerably. He looked around to see a small man dressed as a worker would be standing just a few yards away. Sam shouted over but the man seemed to ignore him. Then, the small man turned around and moved silently through a closed door.

Sam told the foreman and even entered the sighting into the daily report sheet. The next day he was interviewed by curious senior members of the maintenance team as he was unwilling to go anywhere near the Screen Room and was quite disturbed. Whilst Sam was describing the figure one of the older officials piped up, 'That sounds like old George, he used to work here but he's dead now'.

It seemed George had worked at the power station in the early 1940s and did the same job that Sam was doing on the previous night. After word got out it was soon discovered that several other workers had glimpsed the ghost in various parts of the plant.

Galleries of Justice

In 1448, King Henry I gave a charter to the town of Nottingham. The town was to be forever separated, divided and utterly exempt from the county. Nottingham was to be a county itself and not a parcel of the county of Nottingham. The King's Hall was the County Hall or Shire Hall and stood on the site of the present structure. It is still in the county and outside the town. Assizes and quarter sessions were held here. The knights of the shire were selected to serve the county in Parliament. The dungeons deep below the present building date back to the very early years of the original Saxon settlement, and were in use well before the Norman Conquest.

Entrance hall where a ghost descended the old staircase.

The rebuilding of the Shire Hall began in 1770. There had been discussion that that the building should be sited in the market square on high buttresses with the stalls underneath. However, the new building was eventually decided upon and would go up on High Pavement. It is interesting that the hall has occupied the same site for nearly 500 years and has seen many changes. Today it is known as National Centre for Citizenship and Law (NCCL) Galleries of Justice and serves as one of Nottingham's leading tourist attractions. The staff have worked hard in recent years to turn the galleries into a centre for the study of citizenship and the law, with many fascinating exhibits from the HMS Prison Service Collection.

There are said to be many ghosts lingering here. An area known as The Pits can have unsavoury effects on some visitors. Some suddenly just get a panic attack and have to get out, and others will feel stifled by an oppressive atmosphere and in extreme cases nausea may set in. Some visitors have claimed to see black shadows flitting about, heard feet storming along empty corridors and even been violently pushed by unseen hands.

In the courtroom there have been loud rapping sounds, awful groans and a dark figure appearing up on the balcony. The criminal court might even reverberate to the agony of those condemned to be branded — the red hot fire and brands were kept in the room where they were being tried. One can only imagine the poor wretch's fear when the verdict 'guilty' was pronounced. Is it any wonder that some people pick up on such terrible suffering that must have left its mark on the atmosphere?

The unsettling atmosphere in the exercise yard is quite palpable.

A rough-cut inscription to a criminal condemned for 'housebraking'.

A grim bed: this room seems still to carry the pure hopelessness of those who existed here.

In the chapel it has been claimed that an invisible entity sometimes touches the unwary and that stones have been thrown at visitors. A large crucifix is sometimes violently thrown across the room. The elegant entrance hall is said to have three comparatively placid spectres who periodically appear for just a second or two: a man wearing a military-type tunic, a petite lady and a Victorian 'toff'. The cleaning staff are quite used to hearing mysterious footsteps in unoccupied parts of the building when the museum is closed and it is not uncommon for doors to slowly open then slam shut of their own volition.

One member of staff told my researcher an anecdote involving members of the Nottingham Civic Society. Many years ago, before the Shire Hall was converted into the museum you see today, small private parties would be given access from time to time to explore the seemingly endless corridors and grim cells hidden behind the façade of carved stone and grand pillars. The story goes that one party split up and one young woman found herself in the corridor housing the main cells, and decided to explore the end cell – the condemned cell. A commonly reported physical phenomenon is doors suddenly shutting and becoming solidly jammed. This is what now happened to our visitor.

She was exploring the room for some time before she noticed that she was no longer alone! She tried to leave but the door would not open. Elsewhere, the rest of the team were busy looking into the nooks and crannies of this fascinating building – too far away to hear her, until she started to scream. Desperate now to get out of the room, she looked around: the thing was still there, quietly watching her. By this time the rest of her party had found the room and were trying to open the door. Nothing would move it. Surmising that it must have locked itself, they went to fetch the night watchman, who was in the main hall several levels above them.

All this time the sounds coming from the cell became more desperate. Even the night watchmen's keys could not open the door, and many attempts were made to force it open until it finally released itself. The 'something' inside the room had disappeared. The poor woman was helped upstairs and given a soothing cup of tea. She then told the mystified group why she had been hysterically screaming for them to get her out.

She had not been immediately aware of anything untoward in the room until the door closed. She turned and saw, sitting on the iron framework bed, a translucent woman in a wedding dress. Records show that a young bride was executed many years ago after killing her husband on their wedding night: she had become obsessed with the idea that he was infatuated with her sister.

The condemned cell is a morbid room even now. Sited right alongside rooms holding felons who may be a guest of the Her Majesty's Justice for anything from a couple of days to many months and even years, the poor souls found in the end cell knew only that they had a finite length of time left. The identities of the various phantoms remain a mystery but with all those who have passed through, been incarcerated and executed it is probably no surprise that so much psychic residue remains.

At one time the scaffold was erected at the front of the building where several hundred baying onlookers would gather to watch another miserable wretch 'swing'. In later years the condemned were allowed some privacy as the scaffold was positioned in the exercise yard. They would then be interred in the unhallowed ground with a sack of quicklime to speed up decomposition. The bones are still beneath the grim paving stones to this day. At night, a dark figure has been seen in the yard that disappears whenever anyone investigates.

Residents on Cliff Road, which overlooks the rear of the building, have made it known to museum staff that they have seen grim-looking figures shuffling about late at night in the area where prisoners would gather in order to start the long journey on the River Leen to London and the transport hulks waiting to take them to Australia. The laundry and female prison sits directly above the Loggerheads public house (one of the only remaining historical building in the Narrow Marsh area). Prisoners were rumoured to do laundry in exchange for victuals, and there is some evidence of caves linking the two sites, long since blocked up. The owners of the Loggerheads report continued activity and the same kind of phenomenon as plagued the previous tenants. A soldier in First World War uniform has been seen standing in front of a memorial wall plaque dedicated to the local lads who lost their lives in that war.

Nottingham ghost researcher Louise Marriott has made many useful contacts and is well known to the museum staff at the Galleries of Justice. She has visited the place many times and even spent a night or two there with ghost hunters attached to renowned research team UK Paranormal. During one all-night study, many anomalies were logged. In a part called 'the Dark Cell', one researcher, Lara, felt an uncanny pressure at the top of her head and heard an unexplained metallic sound from an empty cell opposite. Mark saw a strange luminous effect in The Burning at the Stake Room. Sue felt an ache down her left arm and neck and Anji felt dizzy and nauseous for no rational reason. In one of the cells a rapid drop in temperature was felt: when tested it was established that a drop of 7 degrees Centigrade had occurred.

Louise and her sister, Samantha, arranged for us to visit one sunny Saturday morning in June 2006. Although Higher Pavement is a stones throw from the busy shopping streets it is unusually quiet, almost eerie. Whilst chatting idly to one of the museum assistants I spied a dark figure wearing a 'bum freezer' type frockcoat and wing collared shirt with cravat move swiftly near the stairs. I casually asked Samantha if she had seen anything: she had not. I then asked the museum assistant if he knew of such a figure. It was then explained there are several actors in period dress who conduct tours around the building: I thought I had seen a ghost!

We were given the freedom to wander the endless corridors and take whatever photographs we needed, and later chatted to Margaret in the café, who knew a few tales. On entry to the criminal court I jolted: there was a lifelike dummy of a judge complete with robes and wig! The place was already giving me the jitters. I do not profess to be sensitive to psychic influences but admitted to feeling strong changes in atmosphere and an unsettling feeling in certain areas of the place.

One is constantly reminded of the suffering that has taken place here. The wooden scaffold hangs over the men's exercise yard and everywhere there are exhibits of various instruments of the law that have been brought together from the HM Prison Service Collection. Here we have the hangmen's box that preceded him by train to each of his appointments, inside it his list of weights for judging the drop, as well as the actual rope. Elsewhere leg irons and other restraints hang from the walls of the condemned cell and a poignant box full of objects poor wretches swallowed in the hopes of taking their own lives sits alongside costumes and books listing those sent for transportation. Women condemned to the colonies were forced to leave their children behind, and the enlightened society that no more wanted to see the mother hanged for stealing bread to try to feed them also provided schooling for the children. This was little more than a workhouse. Here you can see the books that speak to us through the years of these sad, desperate lives. The gallery even displays a rare surviving gibbet. Looking at it I could imagine it hanging above a busy crossroads, the felon's corpse left to rot as an example to everyone else of what awaited those tempted onto the wrong side of the law.

A smell of death seemed to hang around in the dank cellars; I found the place very oppressive. UK Paranormal assured me that activity here is not limited to the hours of darkness alone. The sound of men speaking in Old English has been heard following team members in broad daylight as they walked through the silent corridors making the building safe for the mediums and investigators later that night. Audio recordings have been captured of a large group of people entering an area known as the 1833 Cells: investigators only yards away heard nothing until they replayed the tape. And the sound of the large, metal-studded cell doors slamming shut has been heard reverberating around the building when no human hand can have been responsible.

Bell Inn: The Pub With No Ghost

My researcher Louise Marriott spends many a happy hour in this quiet oasis in the Market Square and was intrigued when the landlord claimed to run the only pub in Nottingham that didn't boast any kind of paranormal activity. She was pleasantly surprised to find staff not talking of phantom monks, not talking of ghastly highwaymen and not talking of other ghoulish wretches roaming the many corridors of what has been established to be the oldest standing inn in Nottingham. An overnight investigation was organised and it soon became apparent that the Bell Inn is, in fact, ghost free.

UK Paranormal experts descend into cellars at The Bell. Left to right: Phil 'Dobbo' Dobson, Samantha Marriott and Mike Driscoll.

The building itself has been traced back to the 1400s, and is believed to have been the site of the refectory for the Carmelite Friars who were granted the lands between the Bell Inn and Nottingham Castle in 1276. The inn stands on a labyrinth of natural and manmade caves and there is evidence that these were extended by the Carmelites and wells sunk so the waters could be used for brewing beer.

Landlord Brian Rigby is especially interested in uncovering the history of the pub and takes guided tours into the first level of caves where one can see evidence of the friars' work and the remains of a cock-fighting pit. He hopes one day to be able to open up more of the lower reaches of the cave system with its twisting corridors, extensive Victorian port cellars and evidence of the area's ongoing use for the brewing and bottling of alcohol well into the early twentieth century.

Newdigate House

Many buildings on the portion of Castle Gate between the castle and Maid Marion Way are said to harbour ghosts: indeed, on the regular ghost walk events much of the tour involves anecdotes of the ancient buildings on this quiet thoroughfare. The best known is that of Newdigate House. Its most famous resident was the Duc de Tallard, a great soldier-statesman who, after his defeat by the Duke of Marlborough at the Battle of Blenheim in 1704, was incarcerated here. He remained here until 1712, when he was ransomed back by the French. His time in Nottingham had been so enjoyable he promised to come back and maybe he does.

Castle Gate. Many buildings here are haunted, Newdigate House being the most famous.

The ghost here is unseen but heard. Usually just before daybreak unmistakably French words emanate from the parlour: the voice is assumed to be the psychic residue of Duc de Tallard. Footsteps are heard in the hallway and the sound of billiard balls clicking on a non-existent table.

Queens Medical Centre

Places where there has been much anguish often seem to retain haunting phenomena. Hospitals, particularly the older buildings, have all got stories of ghosts. Very often it seems to be a revered matron, unwilling to depart her tireless devotion to her patients and nurses who she would be firm but fair with.

The vast Queens Medical Centre has a ghost. On night shifts, the nurses have a designated rest room on each ward so they may lie down for a break in the early hours of the morning. There is a rest room in one part of the building with something of a reputation. Some of the nurses avoid it due to a 'feeling' about the place. There have been instances where nurses have nodded off in the room to find themselves being vigorously aroused by a black nurse who utters, 'C'mon dear, time to get back to work'. Enquires have found that no one recognizes the mysterious nurse.

In a similar small rest room in another part of the hospital a night nurse was awoken from her slumber by awful screaming. She leapt up and ran into the darkened ward: the patients were sound asleep and nothing was amiss. She put it down to a nightmare and returned to try to get back to sleep. She was again awoken from a fitful doze by screaming: a female voice shrilled,

Queens Medical Centre, a busy hospital where a long-departed nurse visits in the night.

'Please help me, for the love of God please help me'. The terrified nurse tore out of the rest room and into the ward – again, everything seemed quite normal. Baffled, the nurse went to the next ward and asked a colleague if she had heard anything. She had not. The dazed nurse stayed up for the rest of the night.

It came to light that at least two nurses had seen the top half of someone wearing a grey hooded robe-type garment pass the staff room window late in the night. On both occasions on investigation no one was found.

Wilford Ambulance Station

The ambulance station on Wilford Road had a mysterious phantom, shadowy but clearly evident.

In 1973 two ambulance men watched bemused as a small shadowy man walked into a toilet. They decided to follow as the public were not allowed to be in this part of the building. When they entered they were astonished to find no one there. There were periodic footfalls and doors violently opening of their own volition. On rare occasions an atmosphere of impending doom would be evident.

One man had a peculiar experience late one evening. He was in the ambulance cab when he saw a black shadow moving to his side. He assumed it was his partner and began to talk about a 'shout' earlier that day. On receiving no answer the man stepped down from the cab and realized his colleague was in the telephone room: he was alone in the vehicle bay.

Mansfield Road

Mansfield Road, the part between Forest Road East and Shakespeare Street, is a popular shopping area. Being close to the university campus and residences many students visit as there are several thrift clothes shops, retro shops and second-hand booksellers. There is also a couple of excellent pubs. The present author admits to always going there if in Nottingham.

In the mid 1970s a shop that dealt in antique weapons was the focus of ghostly visitations for some reason or another. The large premises, built in 1800, had three small cottages at the rear (recently demolished to make way for new student accommodation). One evening, the dealer, Mr Shaw, was in one of the cottages that had been used as a restoring workshop when he felt he was not alone; he looked around and was stunned to see a vague figure in the corner. It was a young girl of around ten years old. She had a drab dress with a white apron and tatty shoes but, most unsettlingly, no hands! Mr Shaw backed off in shock as the figure faded leaving a strong sense of sadness.

Another occasion involved one of the staff, Mr Kicks; he was in another cottage used for storage when the air temperature suddenly dropped. There was no one there but he felt a definite presence and a feeling of sadness permeated the room. It became so intense he had to get out.

During work to improve security at the shop an electrician was engaged to install a burglar alarm. He was mysteriously locked in the room where the control panel would be housed on two occasions and felt unsettled also.

Mr Shaw encountered the phantom again nearly a year later. It was in the same cottage: this time he noticed a drawing on the table that he or no one else knew anything about. He 'felt' that the ghost wanted to draw his attention to the sketch and for him to act on it. An exorcism was later performed which stopped the visitations, but an adjacent bookshop may have inherited them. The owner's son lived in the flat above for four years and hated going through the place at night, feeling particularly unsettled on the first floor landing just outside the flat. He was adamant some kind of presence haunted the corridor all the time he lived there and took to closing his eyes and bolting through the unseen presence. The proprietor explained that the shop goes icy cold at two o'clock every afternoon to this very day. This had been noticed a couple of times by my researcher, Louise, but as it was a hot summer she had put it down to the place being air conditioned – it was that cold!

Further up Mansfield Road is the Sherwood Manor pub and restaurant. Set back in pleasant grounds the pub is popular in summer with an outdoor area for children and picnic tables for the adults. A mysterious dark, indefinable figure haunts this inn. It wears some kind of floppy hat and a frock-type coat and is mainly encountered in the cellar, quite often by draymen delivering ale. Theories include the idea that the ghost is of the man who had the place built as a grand residence but died before it was completed. On the whole he seems innocuous but there have been instances where entire crates of beer have been moved and empty crates thrown about in the cellar.

Ye Olde Trip to Jerusalem

This very popular watering hole is to be found on Brewhouse Yard, a pathway at the side of Nottingham Castle. It purports to be England's oldest inn, built in 1189. At one time it was said to be a meeting-up point for the men preparing to go on crusade and the area's use as a brewery stretching back to Roman times would seem to support this. Although the building itself doesn't date back that far there is evidence that the area itself was being used for brewing beer for the castle residences from the time of the Norman Conquest and possibly long before: the proximity of the River Leen would, indeed give some credence to this story. Not only is the place popular with the tourists but locals treat it almost as a regular meeting place too. During my researches for this book I was forced to spend many hours there soaking up the atmosphere and I noted seeing the same characters quite often.

The building is a labyrinth of winding walkways and low ceilings with many small rooms, nooks and crannies. Much of it is built into the sandstone and the cavernous cellars are quite remarkable indeed. One popular brew that regulars (and my researcher Louise) enthuse about is, 'Cursed Galleon'. This is only for the seasoned drinker! It can have a peculiar effect on the unwary! This ale got its name from a notorious artefact that is to be found in a small upstairs room. It is an ancient dust- and cobweb-covered galleon of some eighteen inches in length. It rests above the small counter, hanging from the ceiling in a glass case. There is a legend that anyone who even touches it will suffer dire consequences: they are accursed. None of the staff will touch it, but in order for it to be preserved in its glass case someone must have! A medium I know laughed at the tale and handled it: her car was involved in an accident and she was quite badly hurt.

In one of the little rooms the scents of lavender and rose water suddenly come and go. Glasses fly off shelves and, even odder, the sound of breaking glass is heard but nothing is seen when staff go to clear it up. UK Paranormal have investigated the building several times and have caught audio recordings of glasses moving across the bars, furniture moving and the sound of a single female scream in a long-since bricked-off room in the cellars. They have also encountered apparitions, the first being what was described as a very handsome blond gentleman in the coarse woollen garments of many centuries ago. The viewer described the garments as looking if they were dyed with natural colours. The apparition appeared suddenly behind another team member as they gathered at the main bar for the team's traditional cup of hot soup at about 4 a.m.

Interestingly the team saw another apparition, this time more unsettling, which has been verified by another locally-based investigation group, EMGIG (the East Midlands Ghost Investigation Group), who quite independently reported it appearing to one of their member some four months later. Two UK Paranormal team members were positioned against the far wall in the inner courtyard when their attention was caught by a movement in the window of the Rock Lounge above them. Looking quickly at each other to make sure it was visible to them both they watched what they describe as a figure, dark like tar with no discernable features, moving very quickly across the room. This same alarming apparition had also been encountered by an ex-landlady who was unlucky enough to be mopping the floor early one morning as it made its way down from the Rock Lounge, through the main bar past her and through the (locked) front door into the street. Subsequent visits by UK Paranormal included extensive experiments to try and record the phantom but it has only been seen once more, this time coming from the area of the private quarters near the kitchens and, again, disappearing down the stairs to the main bar.

In the cavernous cellar the darkish figure of a man storms the many dank caves. He is heard

Ye Olde Trip to Jerusalem. Built into the castle motte this ancient inn has a number of ghosts.

Brewhouse Yard in 1885: only the row of cottages remains. The chimney of the pub is on the middle right.

A black figure has been seen at the upper windows.

A ghost in crinoline has been seen near the cellar.

more often than seen but usually inspires witnesses to go upstairs quicker than they came down! One visitor saw a lady in a crinoline dress walk into the cellar and disappear.

A party of five tourists asked if they could view the cellars. Staff are used to such requests and if not busy they will show the interested visitor. On this occasion the entire party saw a pair of seventeenth-century figures walk into a wall! One visitor, finding all the seats taken, settled himself in the circular alcove directly opposite the main bar whilst his partner went to get drinks (I am assured he was quite sober). He was idly gazing out from his snug spot at the many foreign banknotes that plaster the walls of the main bar when suddenly everything changed. Although this was mid-winter and it was dark and pouring with rain outside, he found himself looking at a hot summer scene. The building in front of him had disappeared, to be replaced by a large expanse of dry, yellow grass stretching away to a river with fields replacing the road and the college buildings. He heard the sound of a horse approaching and a young man, scruffily dressed in little more than rags, ran in and hid behind a large kiln-like structure that was beside him. This vision lasted for only a second but had a lasting effect on the young man.

There is another timeslip incident to relate – this time from outside the building. A gentleman standing looking toward the college over the road was surprised to see it disappear, the expanse of the road and bus terminus being replaced by rolling fields. It is impossible not to sense the long history of this enchanting inn; if in Nottingham, go to the 'Trip': just ask a passer-by, everyone knows where it is.

The cursed galleon; only the foolhardy dare touch it.

TWO

SHERWOOD FOREST

No book on ghostly Nottingham would be complete without reference to the sprawling Sherwood Forest, a beautiful and at times enigmatic area. The name 'Sherwood' was first recorded in AD 958. Apparently it means 'woodland belonging to the shire'. Many communities existed with smallholdings, and later the forest was popular with the Normans. King John was a very keen rider and hunter and even had a hunting lodge built, the remains of which are surprisingly still in evidence near Clipstone.

In the thirteenth century, Sherwood covered a fifth of the county of Nottingham, some 100,000 acres. The Great North Way and the London to York road ran through the huge forest. Travellers would be on constant guard against robbers who took advantage of the dense woodland for cover. These characters lived outside the law, which is where the term 'outlaw' originated. This period would have been the time of that infamous hero Robin Hood, portrayed in countless films and TV series.

Prince John was left to look after his ailing brother, Arthur. Prince John was an evil man who wished to rid himself of the young prince and thus declare himself heir to the throne. To help him achieve his aim he placed the shire of Nottingham under the protection of his friend, the Sheriff of Nottingham. It was not long before the poor were reeling under the hard taxes imposed by the prince, but there was one nobleman who remained faithful to the King Richard, Robin of Locksley, who, as the leader of a band of freedom fighters outlawed by Prince John, robbed the rich and gave to the poor.

Lady Marian Fitzwalter (Maid Marian) was a childhood friend of Robin Hood and would often help his cause and would constantly hamper the evil doings of Prince John and the Sheriff. For me personally the long running television series of the late 1950s and early 1960s was the most enjoyable of all the dramatizations – the stunningly handsome Richard Greene as Robin Hood, Bernadette O' Farrell as Maid Marion, the ever-sinister Donald Pleasance as Prince John and the reliable Alan Wheatley, who portrayed the Sheriff with just the right measure of menace. Today there is mild controversy as to the origin of the legendary figure, who probably did exist but was unlikely to be the dashing hero we have come to know and love.

THE TRUNK. MAJOR OAK.

The Major Oak Tree.

The argument continues that he was based in Yorkshire not in Nottinghamshire: he was born in Wakefield, lived in the large Barsdale Forest and died at Kirklees Priory, the popular theory being that Robin was brutally murdered by the prioress of Kirklees. Some say his grave is somewhere under the thick undergrowth. However, the present author leans towards him being a Nottinghamshire man – of course he was!

In medieval times the forest was a productive resource for timber used for building. Stripping of oak bark and charcoal were used in tanning leather, and acorns would be gathered for feeding pigs and cattle. In the twelfth and thirteenth centuries various Christian monastic orders established monasteries within the woodland on land granted to them by the crown, Thurgaton, Rufford and Newstead being three of them. After Henry VIII closed all the abbeys some of the larger estates fell into private ownership and much of the land was used to build country houses.

During the Victorian era, the forest would become a tourist attraction with the huge Major Oak Tree as a popular stop off. This massive tree is nearly 53 feet high with a trunk diameter of 33 feet and a spread of 92 feet. It is thought to be 1,000 years old and it has been claimed that Robin Hood hid in its hollow trunk. During the First and Second World Wars, the forest was thought an ideal training facility for the military, so the Ministry of Defence commandeered a large portion of the land. It is now known as The Sherwood Forest Country Park, attracting many visitors. There is a park ranger service and information centre and one can buy booklets and the obligatory Robin Hood merchandise. There is also a large holiday complex with log cabins and a huge swimming pool inside a Perspex dome.

Forests and woods can be a little spooky sometimes, particularly after dusk. There is a certain type of entity known as a nature spirit or elemental that tends to favour woodland areas. Fairies may too, although not quite the dainty little things with fluttering, gossamer wings of popular imagination – more like an essence, unseen but sensed. Children might see them as little fine misty forms, but they do not trust grown-ups or anyone who does not believe in them, and so prefer not to show themselves very often.

Sherwood Forest has quite a spectacular nature spirit; it is known as, 'The Green Man'. This phantom is only seen at night, very often by courting couples. Those who behold it are struck by the sheer size of the thing. He is 7 feet tall, has scruffy long hair and a rough beard and wears a long green coat. He strides silently along the less used pathways, preferring the more dense woodland. Interestingly he bears quite a striking resemblance to one of Robin Hood's merry men, Little John!

Perhaps this figure has been created as a 'thought form'. Highly psychic individuals could envisage an image of something or someone and in some way that image is retained for others to experience or witness. How many have visited Sherwood Forest and not thought of the legends of these heroes? Maybe even all the merry men and even Robin Hood have been 'created' by the countless visitors and fans of the stories.

There may be another ghost who appears in the vicinity of the Major Oak. An elderly couple were spooked by a large, dark apparition here one dark evening just a few years ago.

A fanciful Edwardian postcard view of Robin Hood and Maid Marian in Sherwood Forest.

The picturesque village of Barnby Moor on the edge of Sherwood Forest, seen here in the 1920s.

The Green Man: Courting couples would be well advised to stay away from the denser parts of Sherwood Forest after dark!

THREE

NORTH OF NOTTINGHAM

Many regions of Great Britain lay claim to having a phantom hound or two wandering around at dusk. Indeed, Sir Arthur Conan Doyle found his inspiration for the terrifying beast in his *Hound of the Baskervilles* from such a supernatural creature: its name was Black Vaughan, a legendary creature from Kington in Worcestershire. Locally there are various names for these canine phantoms: Black Shuck, Shug, Galleytrot, Shag and Shuck.

John Harries, author of *The Ghost Hunters Road Book*, was inspired to research ghosts after an experience he had whilst serving in the RAF. He was stationed in north Norfolk. On this evening he had been to a village a few miles away for a beer or two (no more). It was customary in the outlying regions for bicycles to be provided for RAF personnel and he was riding along on his way back to the air base as dusk set in. He then noticed a large black dog loping to his left that seemed to keep up with him despite being at a steady trot. John carried on and kept glancing at the huge hound. It did not seem bothered by him, almost dismissive. John pedalled fast down a hill but the dog stayed with him until he reached the guard hut: he stopped and watched the dog carry on into the distance. Later he heard of Black Shuck who haunts various paths and lanes in the area: was it the old phantom who had been his travelling companion?

On the Old Trent Road at Beckingham, from where the water meadows are to the church, is the stretch of quiet road where a phantom hound is likely to be seen. It often forms in the churchyard then lopes off along the lane and turns off near an old boatyard where it crosses the swampy water meadows before fading away. It is thought the ghost was a guard dog who belonged to the lord of the manor in the seventh century. Apparently it deserted him to follow a missionary priest who came to convert the villagers: when it died the priest buried it in the churchyard as his first convert.

Like all such spectral black hounds, one might be prudent to give them a wide berth. There is a tale of one foolish local farmer from nearby Gainsborough who encountered the beast and rather than leave it alone kept standing in its path and goading the hound. The dog tried to walk around but he kept blocking its passage. The dog's eyes intensified to red orbs and it bared its huge fangs in an attempt to warn the man. He collapsed and fell in a dead faint. The farmer was found the next morning talking gibberish and almost totally paralyzed: he never recovered.

Clifton

The grand Clifton Hall, still a private residence, was the home to the Clifton family for nearly 600 years. They owned the villages of South Clifton and North Clifton and many acres of land; they also possessed a harbinger of doom. The River Trent was home to a monstrous fish that would sometimes occupy the water meadow just below the church that serves both villages. There, the huge fish would splash about and make a nuisance of itself. Many of the villagers were terrified of the thing and kept well away from this part of the river. An appearance of the sturgeon-like fish of some 5 feet in length announced the imminent death of the present head of the Clifton family. Once the event was marked by the slow peal of bells from the church, the fish would then turned tail with a big splash and head upstream.

Scrooby

With all the bypass roads available today we often drive around rather than through quaint little hamlets and villages, blissfully unaware of their existence. Such a place is Scrooby on the old Great North Road from London to Edinburgh. In the seventeenth century it was not uncommon to pay tolls on busy roads. This was in order to finance any repairs and general maintenance that was necessary. Like today, the idea was less than popular and it could affect one's income drastically if engaged in a lot of travelling. The toll keeper, usually a hefty character who was unlikely to be intimidated by irate travellers and was able to deal with those trying to avoid payment, lived in a cottage by the tollgate. Sometimes it was a very dangerous job: there was always the likelihood of local wretches robbing the toll keeper.

In 1779, on a dark winter's night, local rogue John Spencer (after a skinful of harsh ale) decided to rob the toll keeper's cottage. He quietly gained entry into the dark and silent house. The rogue soon found the heavy iron toll box full of coppers and hefted it on to his shoulder, but the toll keeper, William Yeadon, heard movement and ventured downstairs. He lunged at Spencer: the box fell as a violent struggle ensued. The fight resulted in the toll keeper and his wife being murdered: Spencer bludgeoned them both with a hedgestake. Nearby residents, disturbed by their desperate screams, ran over and caught Spencer and put a call out for the authorities. After his trial at Retford, John Spencer was taken back to the cottage and hanged at the side of the Great North Road; he was then left to rot in rusty chains with the hedgestake roped to his hand.

A dark and mysterious figure in a long coat has been seen near the old cottage on the side of the road. It has been mistaken for a hitchhiker by passing motorists. One man had a particularly unsettling experience in 1952. After missing the last bus to Retford he had got a lift as far as Hawks Nest and then began to walk in the hope of finding a sympathetic motorist. In those days there was little traffic, so it was unlikely. As he approached Scrooby he noticed a small cottage that was unfamiliar. As a light was on downstairs, he stopped and watched a dark figure silently moving in the parlour of the cottage. The man started to walk, then jumped as an awful scream emanated from the building – he stopped and watched as the light went out, and a man staggered out clutching his bleeding head. There was then another scream, a female. Then, a lumbering figure carrying something heavy ran out and vanished into the wooded areas at the rear. The man panicked and ran into the fields: in his haste he lost his direction and eventually returned to the same spot, but the cottage was gone!

He eventually got home and stayed up all night. In the morning he reported the matter to the police. He had witnessed a robbery and assault. Of course, the investigations found no such cottage, and the matter was dispensed with by the authorities. However, the man was adamant and by talking to locals found out about the toll gate murders. He had experienced a psychic replay of the terrible events of that dark night in 1779. No one knows whether the apparition on the side of the road is that of the toll keeper or of John Spencer. All that is known is that the ghost exudes a depressing atmosphere.

Worksop

Quite near to the old priory at Worksop is a popular walking place and beauty spot known as Canch Walk. A stream called The Canch is ideal for dogs to splash about in, and in summer it is ideal for children to wade in or play with fishing nets trying to catch an elusive 'tiddler' or two. At night the place is less inviting. The thick overhanging trees and dark water create a sinister scenario. One may encounter the Canch ghost if unwise enough to be here around 11 p.m. One experience reported in 1906 tells of a well-observed encounter by a person who acted sensibly when faced with the supernatural.

It was an icy, moonlit January night with a frost everywhere. The young man left the path and went over to the frozen iron rail at the deep part of the stream to see if the Canch was frozen: it was not. As he moved away he saw a person approaching from the direction of the church. It was a woman in drab clothing and wearing a thick shawl over her head; as she got nearer, the man realised she made no sound on the hard ground. He felt a tingly sensation as he tried to look at her darkened face, and then the woman was gone – vanished into thin air. The young man, although unsettled, had noted this vital description.

Who the phantom was is unknown. Some assume it may be connected with the old priory as such places often have a haunting. Another possible explanation relates to a woman whose body was found floating in the water in the late 1800s. Also nearby is an affable ghost locally dubbed, 'The Blue Lady'. She is seen in the priory churchyard near the twelfth-century gatehouse.

Sometimes she will rest from her nocturnal perambulations by sitting on a large, low branch on an ancient tree by the path. One has nothing to fear on meeting her and those who do come across The Blue Lady should feel charmed.

Babbington

The site of Babbington Colliery lies three miles north-west of Nottingham. It was opened in 1842 and remained in use until its closure in 1986. A hazardous environment and not everyone's cup of tea, only those who have worked in the mining industry will know of the dry heat, shadowy light and at times claustrophobic conditions. Of course there were many terrible incidents at coal mines resulting in serious injury and often death. Some of these long-departed miners seem reluctant to leave the dark and dank caverns.

In 1954 improvement work was carried out, deepening one shaft and reorganizing the ventilation system. During an afternoon shift five workers were engaged in building a wall to seal off an unworkable section of the mine. While they were having a break, a dark moving shape caught their attention. It was a miner, but not wearing the regulation National Coal Board orange overalls of the time: he was dressed in rough, 'navvy type garb', collarless shirt, neckerchief, old trousers and boots, with a cap on his head. The figure stopped and folded his arms; he then remained silent and prone staring at the partially completed wall. One of the bemused workmen stood up and approached the figure. As he got within a few feet he turned away and disappeared back into the old workings. The workmen felt unsettled and did not feel inclined to follow.

There was an incident in which a solitary figure was seen to enter the cage, (an elevator from the ground to the coal seam), pull the shutters and ascend. This was quite unusual, especially as it seems that when the cage reached the summit there was no one in it! One day a miner was trying to open two heavy gates in one of the old workings; he was having great difficulty in moving the things. As the perplexed miner swore he heard, from the other side of the gates, an echoing voice say, 'I'll give yer a hand'. Then the gates swung open easily, but there was no one on the other side! He was totally alone.

A miner was almost about to finish: it was dawn, although down a mine it is permanently dark. He suddenly felt like he was not alone – and then a man appeared. His features were horribly disfigured. The stunned miner stared in terror as the mute figure strode by and disappeared into the gloom. It was later established that many years earlier a miner was killed in that area whilst operating a cutting machine. These machines are huge beasts and renowned for nasty accidents.

A rare collective sighting once came to light. A group of miners had just finished a night shift. As they arrived at the cage they all observed a man wearing a flat cloth cap and a tatty waistcoat, who looked like a nineteenth-century worker. What was intriguing – and in stark contrast to his overall shabby and coal-streaked appearance – was a fine white silk neck scarf. The fascinated men walked over to him as he had ignored their greetings, but as they got within a few feet, the man faded away. Lying on the grimy floor was the tattered remains of a white silk neck scarf.

At Clipstone Colliery two young miners had a nerve-wracking experience during a shift in 1984. They suddenly found themselves in the company of a miner they did not recognize: not only that, but his outfit appeared to be from the 1930s. The two young men felt their hair rising – it was a ghostly miner, who then leaned over and put its hand on one of the miners' shoulders. They just fled in terror.

There is a belief that phantom miners are unlikely to harm anyone. They are simply lingering where they spent most of their waking lives.

Retford Town Hall

A phantom barrister, it is claimed, inhabits the Town Hall in Retford. This ghost from Victorian or Edwardian times is an uninteractive ghost; he seems unaware of the present and remains within his own dimension in time. He is said to be quite tall and thin, wearing a grey wig and dark gown. He moves unhurriedly around the building, and is usually seen on or around the grand staircase.

Retford Town Hall in the 1920s.

Wellow

Two of the pubs in the village of Wellow are reputedly haunted. The Olde Red Lion has been an inn since 1600. Over the years there have been some changes, the most drastic being the addition of several farm labourers' cottages which were bought and added to extend the inn. Not long after John Henshaw took the pub four people came in early one evening. They ordered drinks and asked for menus before finding a suitably large table. After around twenty minutes they all got up and left. John was confused, as they never said goodnight and two of the party left their drinks unfinished.

At 8 p.m. John received a telephone call. It was one of the ladies from the party who had departed so hastily. She apologised for their actions and then explained that she had seen a scruffy looking man: he was hazy and she knew he was a ghost. He looked like a chimney sweep or a miner. People were walking through him; she was the only person who saw him and it upset her. Bill Davis was a stonemason, a grafter. He would come into the pub at the same time every evening and chose his favourite chair by the fireplace. He liked his pipe and would perform a routine that some found odd but he was something of a character. He would open his oilskin tobacco pouch and select a strip of 'rough cut', then get his pocket knife and cut it up rather than using the traditional method of flaking it with his fingers. He would use his finger (instead of a tamp) to clean out the pipe bowl, then fill it up. Unknowingly he would dirty his face with his hands when he habitually rubbed his face. With his work clothes and cloth cap he did resemble a chimney sweep.

Another time a lady told John that there was a strong psychic presence (or two presences) she 'felt'. John went with her as she pointed out Bill's old chair and the foot of a staircase. John knew nothing to explain the staircase. It would be years later when he found out that a former landlord had fallen down the stairs and broken his neck; he died later as a result.

Minor phenomena such as cold spots and unexplained bumps would sometimes occur. One of the most interesting anomalies occurred after a refurbishment. All the chairs were re-upholstered and re-varnished, but on one chair the varnish on one arm wore down rapidly. Bill has been blamed for this.

There may be another ghost. Former landlord Tony Brown ran the pub for nearly forty years but had just one unexplained experience. It was in the early hours of the morning, when he awoke to see a shadow passing the moonlit bedroom window. He told his wife to come back to bed: there was no reply, so Tony sat up and discovered his wife was sound asleep next to him. He put the bedside lamp on and observed there was no one in the room apart from them.

Two past landlords and various staff have glimpsed a monochrome, hazy image of a young boy in the cellar. A child did fall down a deep well here and drowned, which is thought to be the ghost. Just across the village green is The Durham Ox. Glasses coming off shelves and not breaking, taps turning on causing floods and an ashtray exploding have led many to believe the place is haunted. A former host, Robert Renshaw, found his six year-old daughter chatting in her bedroom. Humouring her, he asked who her friend was; she said she was chatting to the little girl in the corner. Robert smiled and forgot all about it. It was only a few weeks later when his wife encountered a grey, misty child on the landing that Robert began to wonder.

Shortly after Dave and Julie Preston took over the pub in 1990, a series of inexplicable events convinced them of a ghost in the inn. Several customers commented on being tripped by something unseen on a small flight of stairs and a humorous plaque behind the bar just leapt into the air one evening. Later on they both saw the ghost at the same time, although they were in different areas. Julie was in bed with the bedroom door open waiting for Dave to retire for the night. She sensed something was in the room with her, then a white shape flew past the bed and out on to the landing before shooting down the stairs. Dave himself caught a whitish blur out of the corner of his eye; it shot past into the dark lounge and vanished. No one has any idea who the ghostly child might be. Apart from the occasional tantrum the phantom seems amiable and no one has been seriously frightened by it, so it has become like a part of the furniture.

Thorney

Tales abound of highwaymen, 'gentlemen of the road', glorified in books and films as dashing figures in rich outfits upon beautifully trapped mounts. Most of these vagabonds were scruffy, murderous wretches. Such a character was Tom Otter. He terrorized travellers on the Great North Road. If a foolhardy coach driver attempted to fend off Tom Otter he would be bludgeoned with a musket or even shot. He was thought to hide in a large cave near Muskham Bridge. His days were numbered when his hideout was discovered and a posse was formed. He was caught and imprisoned in March 1806. After he was hanged, his miserable body was taken to Byards Leap where a gibbet was erected. He was wrapped in chains and left to the crows.

On rare occasions, the twilight traveller on the quiet lanes around Thorney may see a dark figure on a horse, the chilling ghost of the wretched Tom Otter.

The quaint Strelley church, where the shade of a devout churchgoer wanders the quiet graveyard.

Strelley Church

The oldest part of this delightful church is the lower portion of the tower. The tower grew to its existing height over two centuries with much of the rebuilding carried out in the fourteenth century. The designer and builder of the church, Sir Sampson de Strelley, lies with his wife, Elizabeth, in a striking tomb of alabaster in the chancel He died in 1390. After Elizabeth's demise, further ornate carving was carried out on the tomb we see today. The head of the knight rests on the family crest, a strangled Saracen's head. He holds his gauntlet in his left hand: in his right is the hand of his lady. He wears a sheathed dagger on the right and a sword on the left. The head of the lady has hair trussed at the sides and with a hands on coronet. Round the base of the tomb are fourteen angels bearing shields which at one time were emblazoned. Beneath the tomb there are two graves filled in with rough stones and hard lime mortar.

The nave has octagonal pillars and corbels supporting the inner order of the arches. The pulpit is made up of four old carved oak panels, and has a Jacobean canopy from the late seventeenth century with some sixteenth century Flemish glass that is still in a fine state of preservation – just an ordinary village church. For some reason, the most haunted uninhabited buildings are churches. Any casual visitor alone in a church will indeed soak up its atmosphere. I recall in the early 1970s, whilst staying with relatives in the village of Filby in Norfolk, wandering the country lanes for probably miles and discovering tiny churches in the middle of nowhere. I went into one and rested from the hot July sun. The place was totally deserted and eerily quiet. In those days churches were open from dawn until dusk for those wishing to worship, visit, rest or even do brass rubbings. Of course in the bible a holy site is a place of sanctuary: no such thing in this day and age. No thought of ghosts entered my mind, but on reflection my mind state altered whilst in the small, flint church. Perhaps this might have some bearing on those with relaxed minds being more receptive to psychic influences.

In the churchyard at Strelley is a harmless little wraith, a devout churchgoer named Ettie. It is widely believed locally that she was interred in the graveyard and impatiently awaits her surviving husband. Strange light effects have also been seen within the empty and locked church in the dead of night.

Mattercey Priory

The gaunt ruins of this once proud priory are to be found tucked away in almost total solitude close to the river Idle some half a mile north of the Wetlands Bird & Fowl park near Retford.

Ancient monastic ruins most often seem to harbour some kind of psychic residue: some may experience anomalies, whilst others will remain blissfully unaware. At one notorious ruin in East Anglia I thought I caught a faint religious-type chanting coming over on the breeze: this phenomena has been reported wafting across this bleak ruin on more then one occasion. Is it merely the wind playing tricks or a ghostly replay of a past event? One hardy visitor who went to the place on a cold February afternoon in 1989 was to be convinced that what occurred was by no means a result of an over-active imagination or the wind groaning through the trees.

The lady, from Retford, had visited the old priory periodically in the past. On this outing she had come in order to sketch the ruin in its winter setting. Those who draw or paint will know that it requires a certain level of concentration and that one becomes 'wrapped up' in what one is doing. It will require an interruption of some magnitude to cause the artist to lose their connection with their subject.

The lady was sitting alone as early dusk set in: a weird chanting and the sensation of not being alone had ruined her concentration totally. The light was fading anyway so she thought to gather up her pencils and sketch pad and depart, but the chanting seemed to intensify as she approached the ruin. Then she made out a darkish shape in a recess of one of the walls. In the worsening light she peered and observed what looked like a black robed and hooded figure, it seemed to be aware of her presence. The lady was not intimidated: in fact, she was overtaken by a state of euphoria. Was this really a ghost? She went straight towards the thing but it slowly faded away, leaving behind it the strange chanting which also slowly faded. Then, all that remained was an eerie silence.

Others have heard the chanting but appearances by the dark figure, assumed to be a long dead monk, seem few and far between.

Jenny Butler's Hill, Nottingham Road

On one of the main roads leading out of town the driver will find themselves on Nottingham Road. The area is known for an eccentric widow, Jenny Butler, who met her fate in a number of ways if local legend is to be believed. A far more recent haunting has been brought to my attention by Lisa Mellon:

My father's friend was travelling home late one night along Nottingham Road, Hucknall (towards Bulwell). He had just passed the Bowman (a hotel) approaching Jenny Burton's Hill when a woman suddenly appeared in the road. He slammed his brakes on causing a driver behind him to run into the back of him. Convinced that he had hit the woman, he got out of his car, as did the other driver. When he explained what had made him brake so suddenly, the other driver said she had also seen the woman but although they searched around they found no trace of her. He said the dress she was wearing looked old-fashioned and was buttoned up to the neck and that she looked 'real'. This area is known to local people. Apparently a woman called Jenny Burton was murdered near there and that's how the hill got its name. It's more just a rise in the road now but as you travel over it a bungalow sits high up on the left-hand side showing the level that the hill once was.

FOUR

WEST OF NOTTINGHAM

Annesley

Annesley Hall stands hidden from the busy A608 behind a clump of trees and a ruined church. There is a small pull-in then a gate leading to a track through some woods. After two hundred yards there is a little path on the right that leads to long abandoned stables and housing for the staff. Beyond this stands the now deserted Annesley Hall.

The house has long been the seat of the Chaworth family, who were related to the Byrons at Newstead. Indeed, a young Lord Byron took a shine to Mary, one of their daughters. Her parents found him most unsuitable and stubborn; they actually had to throw him out of the house in a bid to rid them of his persistence. One of the men got a serving wench pregnant. Squire Chaworth thought it prudent to have the girl taken to Northumberland to live with a relative as such a business would cause a scandal. She was well cared for and Mr Chaworth sent money and silver to the address.

Eventually the serving wench gave birth to a healthy boy child. More money was dispatched in order for both mother and baby to have a good start. The relative sent regular letters as the girl could not read or write. There was much delight at Annesley hall when a lock of the child's hair accompanied a letter; all seemed well. A few months later, a groom walking through the Annesley Hall grounds at dusk saw the serving wench in her familiar bonnet and woollen shawl; he was most surprised and called over to her. She totally ignored his attentions. The groom thought she looked most unwell, almost cadaverous. He reported the matter to Mr Chaworth, who lost no time in writing to the relative, an aunt, up in Northumberland.

She wrote back explaining that everything was well and the serving wench and child were quite happy. Mr Chaworth felt there was something not right about the affair, as the groom was educated and unlikely to make up such a story. It was decided to dispatch a steward to investigate. After a long journey the steward eventually arrived at the modest dwelling. He was shocked at what he discovered. The aunt was in a drunken state and there was no sign of the girl or child. After sobering up the drunken wretch she told him that the servant had died. She then sent the child to a workhouse. She had dishonestly pocketed the money Mr Chaworth had sent every week.

Annesley Hall, now abandoned except by the ghosts.

Annesley church; a ghostly cleric haunts these bleak ruins.

What haunts Lord Byron's suite of rooms?

An assistant caretaker resigned after seeing something in these cellars.

It was decided not to take official action as the whole sorry affair and cover-up would come to light. The child was located and re-homed with other, more reliable relatives. It was a while before it was established that the groom's sighting of the mother occurred shortly after her untimely death. The groom had beheld a ghost. It was indeed the mournful wraith that had spurred into action the saving of her beloved child. This is a prime example of an interactive ghost obtaining help from the living. Alas though, the actions did not cease her restlessness and she is still periodically glimpsed out in the gardens.

Another harmless phantom is the beautiful lady with lovely long hair. She forms by a well and sits as if in idle thought whilst brushing her hair. She gently fades if anyone gets too near.

Another apparition, seen quite often, is that of another servant girl. She is sighted in the upper corridor of the staff block standing on floorboards that have long since rotted away. She is said to be the unhappy wraith of a girl whose beauty drew the unwanted attention of a senior butler who plagued her with his relentless advances. It is not known what became of her but the room she slept in is one of the few parts of these enigmatic ruins still intact. Maybe she is held here still by the furnishings and meagre decoration of the room where she would have known so much apprehension and unhappiness.

The current caretaker, Rob Gittins, has had more than his fair share of frights. He uses part of the dilapidated stable block as his office and once saw a coffee mug levitate off a shelf and move across the room towards him in broad daylight. His assistant caretaker resigned on the spot after seeing something that haunts the basement of the main hall once too often. Rob himself refused to enter the basement when UK Paranormal visited Annelsey Hall. They found a very nasty atmosphere lingering in the area.

Closed to the public, the hall has sadly seen more then its fair share of vandalism from people out for a scare at Halloween. The main hall was burnt down when some folks practising witchcraft set a fire on the ground floor. Little of the fine decoration of the main hall still exists, but something unworldly lingers on still. A team member was gently persuaded to leave one of the small rooms in Lord Byron's quarters by unseen hands placed on his back.

The old ruined church is also claimed to harbour a ghost. He is suitably attired in the clothes of a cleric of the distant past. Some think it may be the ghost of James Annesley who would often stroll around the churchyard. This harmless phantom is often reported in broad daylight to jaywalk on the busy road then trudge up the hillock and on into the churchyard.

Arnold

Arnold is to be found south-west of the city of Nottingham. Bestwood Lodge lies in large grounds and cuts an intimidating sight with its gothic flamboyance. In the seventy acres of grounds one might encounter the ghost of the stunningly beautiful Nell Gwynne, probably best known for her acting talents. Her appearances are sometimes heralded by the scent of fresh oranges; Nell was an orange seller in her youth.

The manor was granted to King Charles II, who had an affair with Nell Gwynne. In 1683 it was bestowed to his illegitimate son, Henry, who became the first Duke of St Albans. Another phantom at Bestwood lodge is The Grey Lady. She appears quite rarely but chills the blood of those who may behold her; she is quite solid in appearance and has a long dress of some kind. She has been seen in the vast cellars and near the bar area.

Bestwood Lodge, looking like everything a haunted house should be.

An unseen but unnerving ghost is found in the parkland, often at dusk. Two visitors in the late 1930s were strolling along when they heard a large horse bearing up on them from behind. They both instinctively jumped aside for the mount but there was nothing there. The unseen horse passed them and galloped on into the distance.

In the mid 1970s, two local boys climbed over the fence into the park and were terrified by several white, shrouded figures that glided amongst the trees in pursuit of the trespassers. Of course the ghosts perform the seemingly time-honoured tradition of causing icy chills, doors to slam and chandeliers to swing.

The White Hart, Lenton

A pub that until recently would have been an anonymous haunting has now 'come out' and is considered an 'authenticated' case. The White Hart in Lenton is presently the scene of testing by various experts in the field of ghost research. Looking like an average modern pub it was originally a seventeenth-century farm. In 1809 a Mr George Wombwell bought the place and opened the White Hart Coffee Rooms, which was something of a novelty but a successful one. The site later became a debtors' gaol. Upstairs an ancient leather-stretching machine still exists; work such as this was part of the rehabilitation of inmates. The site became a pub when the gaol closed in 1897 after an Act of Parliament.

Evidence of the White Hart once being a gaol includes its barred windows.

The rusting iron handle on the leather stretching machine.

A relief manager met 'something' on these stairs.

A relief manager, Stuart, recently walked into 'something' whilst descending the office staircase in the older part of the building. It was figure of a man that disappeared as he approached it. In the front part of the building sounds of a child singing and running about have been reported and weird dark moving shadows seen. Someone claimed to have been pushed quite forcefully in the back by an unseen person in the kitchen area. This tight, winding corridor links the older portion of the building (with its debtor cells) to the newer, larger portion. The host, Kim, has not experienced anything but keeps an open mind on the idea of a ghost in the pub. The ghost is believed to be the jailer, a violent character and a rogue who leaves an atmosphere of malevolence behind him.

Palace Theatre, Mansfield

A most unusual apparition, or part of one, has been reported here. The Palace Electric Theatre opened in December 1910. It was the town's first purpose-built cinema. At first there were just silent films until the 'talkies' came about in the late 1920s. Shortly after the Second World War the cinema was closed and the stage enlarged in order to present Music Hall and variety shows. In 1953 the theatre was bought by Mansfield District Council for the princely sum of £11,500. After three years of restoration it reopened as the Civic Hall.

In 1968 the District Council offered a prize of five guineas to anyone who could suggest a new name. It was eventually called The Civic Theatre. In 1997 it was redeveloped yet again at a cost of £2,000,000 and now flourishes. Only once has the queer ghost been seen. A simple pair of bright yellow Wellington boots striding across the stage!

The Admiral Rodney, Calverton

It was my sworn duty to visit personally as many allegedly haunted locations as is possible for this book. The Admiral Rodney pub on Main Street in Calverton was of course on the list. The Marriott twins and I nipped over one Saturday lunchtime in August 2006. Although the pub looks fairly new there has been an inn here since the 1700s. It was built with the name of a hero, Admiral George Rodney, who defeated the French in a skirmish in the West Indies between 1762 and 1782.

A trio of phantoms are said to lurk in the pub. A feisty character dressed entirely in black storms about the place on rare occasions. He thrusts locked doors open and slams them shut with much fury then storms down a corridor into the dining area where he vanishes. His ill-fitting suit seems to suggest 'demob' type garb from after the war. So many pubs have a ghostly regular, someone who probably spent more time in their favourite chair than at home, and no doubt was glad to get away from his moaning wife! An old fellow, still recognized by many, sits near the main door nursing a pint of ale. Apparently he almost lived here for nearly sixty years. He is quite solid and would be easily mistaken for a living person. Last but by no means least is the mischievous Sarah. There is a legend that a tunnel in the pub cellar led to the church and that a serving wench, Sarah, had an affair with the rector. She rarely appears and prefers to play irritating tricks such as turning beer taps off and interfering with the cooling system. The staff are used to her antics and just put up with them.

The Admiral Rodney, one of the many Nottinghamshire pubs with a resident ghost.

The Palace Theatre, Newark

Theatres, for some reason or another, seem to provide the correct conditions for ghostly goings- on. The acting fraternity are often of a superstitious nature and believe in ghosts – many welcome them as a good omen. After a run years ago it was customary to find the theatre owner in order to get paid: sometimes he would be elusive and the phrase, 'When does the ghost walk?' came into being. The Palace Theatre in Newark was built on the site of the old Chantry House. The resident phantom is thought to be that of a woman who was suffering from long bouts of depression and decided to end it all: she committed suicide by jumping off the balcony.

Late one night, a number of stage hands were having a break in the 'Punch and Judy Room'. They were casually chatting away when their attention was diverted to the door leading to the auditorium, which slowly opened fully, and then slowly closed. They sat in silence looking at each other as the other door opened and closed: it was as if an invisible person had wandered through. Mysterious, dainty footfalls are often heard throughout the theatre when it is closed to the public. Mostly it tends to be noticed late at night and frequently it seems centred around the balcony.

The unseen spectre made its presence known to a group of people in the Byron Lounge one evening. The group had arrived early for a private function. As they sat chatting, they all felt something pass them in a hasty fashion. Then, to their utter amazement, they observed footprints appear in the new thick carpet. Like most theatre ghosts, the phantom here is totally harmless, merely a remnant of the past periodically going about its perambulations.

S 17647   Palace Theatre and Appletongate, Newark

Harlow Wood

A brutal murder may be the cause of haunting phenomena on the busy A60 road between Nottingham and Mansfield. Only the keen eyed rambler would spot 'The Bessie Stone', a tiny monument by a ditch quite near to Harlow Wood Hospital. The following words are carved into the stone…

'It is erected to the memory of Elizabeth Sheperd of Papplewick who was murdered on this spot by Charles Rotherham on July 7th 1817, aged 17 years.'

On the night of the murder, a man walked into the Three Crowns Inn. He seemed a suspicious character and no one was interested in the pair of worn ladies shoes he was trying to sell. Later on the same man turned up in Bunny, this time selling a ladies umbrella. Once word of the murder got out, people who had seen the man came forward with their descriptions. He was caught after trying to sell the shoes in Mansfield market place.

Charles Rotherham was tried for murder and was found guilty. He was hanged in Nottingham before a huge gathering. Young Elizabeth (she was affectionately known as Bessie) Sheperd was well liked in the village. Bright and ambitious, she went in search of work in one of the larger houses in the area on the day of the killing. She was successful, and at 6 p.m. left her home to begin her new job. She was dressed in her Sunday best and carrying her umbrella. The drunken Charles Rotherham had recently been thrown out of one pub in the area and had no money left. He spied the well-dressed little Bessie and followed her with the intention of robbing her as she looked well to do. He caught her on a quiet stretch of lane and dragged her into the woods that fringe the roadside. After finding she had no money he hit her: after his drink-fuelled and frenzied attack, Bessie fell dying.

In her memory, the villagers raised enough money for a stone and mason to carve an inscription and have the memorial placed at the scene of the murder. The stone lay for many years as a reminder of the evil men do. In 1956 a vehicle swerved off the road and struck Bessie's stone. A few weeks after there were claims of sightings of a young, well-dressed woman by the road near the stone. Some noticed her umbrella. To this day the ghost of Bessie appears by the road. Some motorists stop for her but if anyone approaches she swiftly moves into the woodland and fades away.

Rufford Abbey

Rufford Abbey is just west of Nottingham. It is now a ruin but attracts many visitors as the architecture remains quite impressive. The ruin stands in huge parkland of some 500 acres and is popular with dog walkers and outdoor enthusiasts.

Lady Arabella Stuart was born in 1575. She had an innocent childhood before becoming a victim of the Tudor power game. As a teenager she was taken in hand by Queen Elizabeth after her parents, Charles Lennox and Elizabeth Cavendish, died at an early age. It was decided to send Arabella to her grandmother, the Countess of Shrewsbury, where she would be safe from harm. After Elizabeth died, King James VI brought Arabella to his court in London so he could keep her safe. She eloped with an Earl's son, William Seymour, which turned out to be a grave misjudgement. The marriage was politically unwise, and the king ordered that Arabella be incarcerated in the Tower of London.

A dark phantom known as the Black Friar still wanders the grim ruins of Rufford Abbey

The feisty Arabella made an ill-fated attempt at escape; she hid her hair under a cloth cap, dressed as a young boy and actually managed to escape the tower. She even managed to stow away on a ship at Dover but was captured and returned to the prison. Lady Arabella Stuart was not executed but died of natural causes at the age of forty. Her preference, rather than add to the many ghosts at the tower, was to return to Rufford Abbey where she lingers to this day. In contrast to the gentle wraith of Arabella is a sinister hooded spectre who exudes pure menace, the ghost known as the Black Friar. As to whom he reflects remains unknown but he was probably a monk. This nasty phantom resembles the morbid 'Ghost of Christmas Yet to Come' from Charles Dickens' classic book, *A Christmas Carol*: a large, black, cowled figure that often appears reflected in mirrors behind an unfortunate witness. The large hood hides the features within but it is known to tilt back the head to reveal a terrifying skull-like face. One man from Edwinstowe encountered the thing in December 1900 and apparently died later from shock.

Those who wander the huge parkland, especially near the paths, might encounter a phantom nanny. As a rule her appearances are restricted to the summer months. She wears black and pushes a pram before here. Finally, an unidentified ghostly effect has been reported in and around the ruins. It is a white, chalky figure assumed to be female, The White Lady. It is a brave or foolhardy person who comes into the parkland and ruins of Rufford Abbey after the sun has gone.

Calverton Hall

The long gone Calverton Hall used to have such a reputation as a place of evil and terror that many would refuse to go anywhere near the place, day or night. It is said animals would not venture near and even birds never flew near the hall. One of the housemaids was very excited at the prospect of her wedding to a young coachman, even though others had told her he was not good enough for her: he was a womaniser and immature, and she should leave well alone. But love is blind, and she paid no heed. Just days before the wedding in 1876, the young coachman jilted her. She was devastated and committed suicide.

Quite soon after, a terrible atmosphere would build up in the hall which usually released itself in slamming doors, footsteps and awful chills. The place soon got a reputation as a haunted house. Late one night, a bus driver saw a woman near the bus stop outside the hall so he slowed down and stopped. She stepped on and went on to the upper deck. When the conductor went up to obtain her fare, he found she was not there.

At one time, a local scout group utilized one of the stables at the rear as a temporary headquarters. At this time the hall was a vicarage. One evening, as the scout leader was locking up, he noticed a lady on the driveway who he assumed to be the vicar's wife. As he drew near he bade her a good evening but she ignored him completely. Then, to his horror, she just disappeared. One winter's night, a local lady had to go past the dreaded place and simply could not muster the courage to pass. Even though she was late for an appointment she did not fancy going by, so instead she waited for someone else to walk with. Eventually a woman caught her eye. She was ahead so the lady ran to catch up – then the woman turned, walked into a wall and vanished.

During the laying of water pipes in 1936, contractors discovered a skeleton near the rose gardens. Pathologists discovered a small hole in the skull which was presumably the cause of death. This adds to the mystery as the maid committed suicide in a bedroom. There is a theory that the body was hidden to avoid a scandal. The vicarage closed in the late 1950s. No one wanted to lease or buy the hall so in time it was decided to pull the place down. No firm in the locality would do it, probably because of the reputation of the place, so a company from London took on the demolition contract. Two men arrived and could not find lodgings so they stayed at the new vicarage nearby.

After a few days in the job the pair arrived at the vicarage a lot earlier than usual. They were unsettled and soon confided in the vicar's wife what had occurred. They were both disturbed from their work by the sound of loud footsteps upstairs. The place was structurally unsafe and no one else should have been in the building, so they decided to investigate. One man ascended the servant's staircase while the other went up the main stairs. They met on a landing and tracked the pacing footsteps to a large bedroom. They opened the door and peered in; there was no one in the room yet the footsteps were quite audible on a floor that had been torn out three days earlier! Then they leapt as the sound of smashing china emanated from the scullery. They fled from the place.

Skegby

A morbid replay type of ghostly vision is said to appear at the fourteenth-century Skegby Hall, near Sutton-in-Ashfield. As well as being a once palatial residence, the hall has served as an Approved School and is now occupied by the County Council Social Services Department.

It was during the lengthy period that the place was a school for miscreants that the sightings were recorded. The vision always appeared in part of the headmaster's rooms. Monastic chants are heard then a funeral cortège forms of robed and hooded monks bearing a coffin. The grim spectacle moves slowly through the rooms and fades out as the dirge-like chanting becomes less and less audible, then a chill silence...

Thrumpton Hall

Thrumpton Hall nestles in the green folds between the M1 and the Ratcliffe Power Station west of Nottingham. Apart from one day a year, when the estate is thrown open to the public for the agricultural fair in May, this little gem has been a jealously guarded secret. My researcher, Louise, had gone along after seeing ferret racing being advertised in the local press and, finding the Hall open, decided to take a poke around.

The Hall dates largely from 1607 and was the home of the Powdrill family – staunch Roman Catholics in an age when Catholicism was a dangerous religion to follow. The house is rumoured to have a priest's hide, which may indicate a turbulent history: in fact, it is rumoured that Father Garnett, one of the main participants in the Gunpowder Plot, was hidden at Thrumpton Hall as he tried to evade arrest.

The tour eventually led down some back stairs to a cool, tiled corridor. A row of bells attached to the wall, once used to summon the staff, lay dormant, their strings now severed. There had been very few people taking the house tour as it was a wonderful, hot bank holiday. In fact it was a relief to get away from the heat and hubbub of the crowds enjoying the fair and Louise had spent most of her tour alone with only her sister for company.

As she came to the bottom of the staircase, her attention was drawn to an ill-lit corridor directly to her left. The rooms and corridors above had been a wealth of antiquities and curiosities from a long-gone age: in contrast, this staircase was a plain, wooden affair and the corridor bare and silent. Louise became aware of a presence she decribed to me later as a man, standing to the left, in the shadows who, although dressed in rough work wear, stained with oil, didn't give the impression of being a member of the estate staff yet was intricately linked with the house. She sensed a very strong wish from him for everyone coming past that corridor to leave the house. This man was tolerating the visitors, yet took pride in their comments about the beauty of the house.

She then thought to ask a guide if the house was haunted. Whisked through back rooms, she was introduced to the current custodian of Thrumpton Hall, author Miranda Seymour. An engaging woman, with a quiet authority, she listened to Louise's enquiries but kindly denied any haunting, and Louise thought it best not to describe her experience. A book caught Louise's eye, Lady Seymour's history of her upbringing in this delightful pile. *In My Father's House* tells the story of George FitzRoy Seymour's struggle to protect Thrumpton. It tells of an almost obsessive love for the house, which he had known as a young boy when living there with his relative, the 10th Lord Byron. Always an eccentic figure, George Seymour took to motorbike riding in his later years and could often be found tinkering with the oily engines, with the same enthusiasm he had shown in all aspects of running the estate – often to be found with the staff, in the fields coppicing woods and clearing the ponds. His last years were blighted by the construction of the nearby power station and he planted stands of trees in the hopes of shielding its concrete towers from the house.

Could this quiet presence in the kitchen corridor be the shade of this man who clearly loved this grand old lady of a house? Could George Seymour still be watching over Thrumpton Hall?

FIVE

SOUTH OF NOTTINGHAM

Netherfield

Netherfield lies some three miles east of Nottingham. At the old disused railway sidings near Jack Bell's Field there are a number of houses with a large residential car park. One family installed a CCTV camera unit after the car park began to be visited by vandals trying to break into cars. Luckily for us ghost hunters the family's recording equipment was set up to capture sound also: they inadvertently captured evidence of a previously unknown haunting.

Muffled voices would come through the sound speakers at around midnight. Attempts at identifying the origin of the voices have been fruitless. Oddly, the voices seem foreign, maybe European. Sometimes there are snatches of music which sound like the music of the 1940s. Intrigued, one member of the family, Kath, decided to carry out some research at the local library and after a lot of wading through books made an interesting if unsettling discovery: during the Second World War there was a POW camp in the area. The interns would arrive by train then group at the large sidings where the houses now stand.

Langar

During the Second World War, the military required airfields from which to send bombing missions over Germany. Some existing airfields were commandeered whilst new ones were rapidly constructed. They were basically one or two runways, a hangar, billets and a control tower. The opening and closing scenes of the 1949 motion picture *12 o'clock High* depict the character Major Harvey Stovall, played by Dean Jagger, wandering the ghostly airfield some years after the war and reliving the sounds and drama of the chaos and endless bombing missions that flew from the airfield. These scenes capture the atmosphere in these long abandoned airfields. Like all old RAF and USAAF (United States Army Air Force) military airbases, they are eerily quiet with the breeze rattling old metal windows at the gaunt control tower. A place of memory that grips the unwary visitor, many of these old airfields are said to be haunted.

Netherfield sidings; here one may hear sounds from the Second World War.

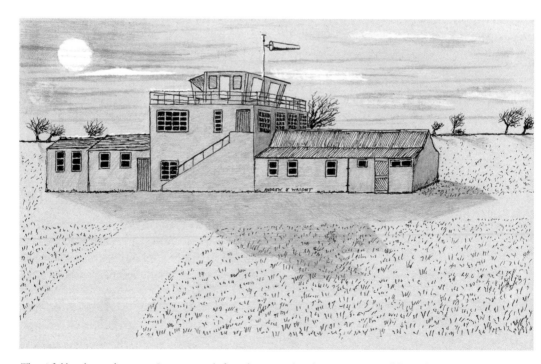

The airfield and control tower at Langar: sounds from the past and a phantom airman still linger here.

Langar Airfield was not fully operational in the Second World War until 1943, when Lancasters flew with 207 Squadron of the Royal Air Force. Like many old airfields, the sites became utilized as storage facilities or industrial units. A firm called Shortland Crafts, a kitchen designer and supplier, took some of the old buildings. One evening in the early 1980s, one of the directors of the kitchen suppliers, Mr Keith Shortland, had just locked up after staying late to catch up on some paperwork. As he drove through the darkening airfield he noticed a tall figure in a uniform approaching swiftly. He braked and shut his eyes, expecting a collision. When the car stopped, Mr Shortland gingerly opened the car door, dreading what he might find, but there was no one to be found. He saw the same figure walk in front of his car some months later; on this occasion he felt that it was an apparition and accepted it as such.

It seems that there were connections with the Royal Canadian Air Force at Langar. During some routine exercises there was an explosion in which several operatives were killed. Is this the phantom that appears on the desolate and bleak old airfield? I must add that in my time I have spent a few night hours in reputedly haunted control towers. I am experienced and used to such situations but admit to finding them all quite atmospheric. It is easy to imagine them when operational and maybe this act might evoke the ghostly sights and sounds.

Colwick Hall

On the southern outskirts of Nottingham, close to the River Trent, stands the palatial Colwick Hall. During the fourteenth century the manor was bought by the Byron family. In 1643 the Byrons sold the hall to Sir John Musters, whose family resided there for many years. During the Reform Bill, Colwick Hall was targeted for attack as the riots spread. John Musters had been a strong opponent of the bill. On 10 October 1832, a large baying mob gathered in the market square in Nottingham. The mob far outnumbered the constables so it was deemed necessary to bring in the 15th Hussars from the Park Barracks to try to restore order.

One group broke away from the affray and made their way to Colwick Hall; they then stormed the place. Some of them got down to the wine cellar, got raging drunk and began piling up any timber, curtains and furniture to create fuel for fires. Paintings were destroyed and nearly all the furniture and fixtures were broken. Mrs Musters, her daughter and a visitor hid from the mob after leaving the hall through the kitchen garden door and hiding in shrubbery in the formal garden. Mr Musters was away at the time. The violent attack had a particularly disturbing effect on Mrs Musters, who collapsed and died just a few weeks later.

Today the building is a hotel. The current house dates from the early eighteenth century. John Carr, the architect, designed it around the original square structure with additional wings. Two ghosts are reputed to haunt the hall and grounds. One is Mrs Chaworth Musters, still suffering from the terror of the attacks of 1832. She is seen cowering amidst the trees and shadows. She has also been recognized in the east wing and was actually photographed by accident when pictures for a brochure were being taken. The other phantom is assumed to be that of Lady Mary Ann Chaworth, who married into the Musters dynasty after her suit to poet Lord Byron was rejected by her family. A mournful wraith, she glides soundlessly along the endless winding corridors.

Colwick Church

A sinister, shadowy figure is said to aimlessly wander the gaunt ruins of Colwick church. Two young couples decided to go there near Halloween in 2001, 'for a laugh'. When they arrived there was a sinister mist blanketing the place creating a suitably spooky scenario. Nina, her boyfriend and his pal decided to investigate but the other girl seemed less than keen to leave the sanctuary of the warm car so she would wait for them there. As they got near the dripping iron gates, Nina idly looked back at the car, which was silhouetted due to the lights from the Greyhound stadium. The other girl appeared to be rocking backwards and forwards as if in an agitated state; it must be because she was scared at being on her own in the car. Nina heard her whining, and then what sounded like weeping. She told the boys she was going back to the car as her friend was scared; they laughed and carried on ahead.

Nina raced back and got in the front passenger seat; she turned around and asked her pal if she was alright: she was fine. When asked why she was rocking back and forth it was explained that she was chatting on her mobile telephone and laughing! So, what had Nina heard?

Newark Cemetery

A phantom airman is said to haunt the tranquil paths of Newark Cemetery. He wanders slowly among the tombstones but fades if anyone curious enough gets too near. There were a large number of servicemen based in the area during the Second World War which will explain why he is often seen around the war graves. He wears a serge, blue/grey RAF-type uniform. Some have surmised he was possibly based at RAF Winthorpe.

Attenborough

England and America have their fair share of haunted battlefields. Weird light effects, sounds and figures are constantly reported around Gettysburg in America. In England the fields where the Battle of Edgehill took place are claimed to have ghostly re-enactments around mid-October.

Phantom soldiers from the English Civil War, Parliamentary troopers with the familiar headgear of a lobster-pot helmet and long swords, periodically appear on the marshy banks of the River Trent near Attenborough. The silent figures astride large mounts fade away near the church. It is believed there was a crossing here before the river was dredged in the nineteenth century. Those who behold them should feel humbled to have seen such a spectacle.

West Bridgford

The leafy suburb of West Bridgford is an area of large houses, shops and small commercial hotels and guest houses. I stayed in one a good few years ago. After finding a fish and chip emporium one evening I idly wandered down towards Trent Bridge and visited the large Lady Bay Inn.

I was blissfully unaware of a ghost said to haunt the large car park outside. The mysterious figure was by no means a regular visitor and I believe has not been seen for many years now. He would appear usually at night; he would form and then glide across the car park in his long coat or cloak, vanishing after just a few seconds. Apparently something would tamper with the pub's light switches but it is unknown if the ghost outside was connected.

The Fosse Way

2,000 years have elapsed since the Romans invaded England and brought their skills to teach us a thing or two about civil engineering. There is a theory that ghosts 'run down' or 'wear out' with time. This theory is put to the test as there are a significant number of Roman ghosts still abroad across Great Britain.

On the busy A46 near the village of Owthorpe it is known that motorists sometimes see a shambling figure by the road heading north towards Lincolnshire. On occasion they will slow down to give the unfortunate a lift but it will vanish into thin air. These types of ghosts are categorized as 'Road Ghosts' or 'Phantom Hitchhikers', on the occasions when the 'person' gets in to a vehicle they usually say nothing and just point ahead. They then vanish and it is sometimes discovered someone was killed at the point of vanishing.

This character, however, dresses in a shabby longish woollen garment of a drab colour and a metal helmet; he carries no spear or shield. He is thought to have come about as a result of a mass killing. Suetonius Paulinus, the Roman Governor of Britain, marched his legion southeast. He then sent messengers to Exeter and Lincoln who took the Fosse Way. Unfortunately the legion and messengers were ambushed and killed by Queen Boadicea and her warriors. A solitary phantom, a psychic reminder of the brutality that existed all too often in Roman times.

Calverton Framework Knitting Museum

This small converted cottage lies off Main Street in a little lane in Calverton. It was built in 1780 and was typical of the small housing in which many framework knitters would have worked. There are many such museums in the small towns and villages where the hosiery industry was the main source of income. However, not all of them have a malevolent, invisible entity that strikes terror into those who happen to be present when it manifests.

The museum is run by enthusiastic volunteers. One dark evening five of the volunteers were sitting at a large table renovating a proposed exhibit when the tranquil atmosphere slowly deteriorated and was replaced by an oppressive, almost claustrophobic feeling. The cheerful chatting ceased as everyone looked around. After a few minutes it was so intense that they all got up, packed the exhibit away and got out. In their haste to leave the lights were left on. One of the volunteers who lived near to the cottage, Mrs Cupitt, went back later to turn them out. She bravely entered and found the horrible atmosphere had lifted and everything seemed quite normal. She has since experienced similar malevolence. Mrs Cupitt is very psychically attuned and is often consulted on local matters of a ghostly nature. Her home is haunted by an elderly man wearing knee breeches and a brown tweed jacket.

Calverton Framework Knitting Museum, where a malevolent presence drove a group of volunteers away.

The haunted house where Mrs Cupitt resides.

An electrician was engaged to work in the old cottage. The job was quite minor so should not take long. After a few days the committee enquired why the job was taking so long. The embarrassed electrician admitted to an unpleasant atmosphere in the place which would drive him out where he would sit in his van for lengthy periods. Several visitors have commented on the horrible change of atmosphere created by the unseen menace.

I spoke to a lady whose front garden is adjacent to the little cottage. She admitted never having seen or heard anything untoward in sixteen years but was sympathetic to the idea of a ghost in the place.

Colston Bassett Church

The old church at Colston Bassett may be home to a mysterious spectre carrying a lighted candle. The small Norman church of St Mary's stands on a hill overlooking the River Smite. Like many small churches, it suffered when the parishioners moved away to the towns in search of work. As the population dwindled the church became abandoned and slowly fell into decay. It is now a gaunt shell. The north aisle has gone and so has the roof; even so, the church stands defiantly against the elements and is a familiar landmark and a monument to those who built it. It will still be there in another 800 years.

In England there are several redundant and abandoned churches in isolated areas that are used by occultists for profane activities. I personally studied one case in neighbouring Lincolnshire over an eight-year period. I observed inverted pentacles, evidence of the sacrifice of small birds, strange symbols daubed everywhere and other rather unsavoury desecrations. The place had a reputation for being haunted by an evil entity that had been 'invoked' by occultists. I spent many nights in the place and admit to experiencing first-hand some very bizarre sights and sounds. Possibly the most unsettling was when I was alone in the church one night. I was almost dozing on my folding chair when a sharp stamping of feet got my instant attention! Whatever it was remained by my side as I sensed I had company although I saw no one.

Thankfully this is not the case at St Mary's church. The twilight visitor brave enough to come up here on a still evening might be surprised to hear the bells peal momentarily. A number of visitors have done and no doubt took it for granted that the wind was the cause. Had they investigated further and examined the tower they would discover there are no bells: they were taken out many years ago. Some claim to hear on the breeze the unmistakable sound of hymns being sung and many have observed a flickering candle at night. Those brave enough to investigate have found just a dark, empty old church.

Gunthorpe

A phantom feline no less is supposed to haunt the water meadows at Gunthorpe village. It is said to be quite large and black. There are a good number of mysterious large cats that live wild in Great Britain. Most commonly panthers, these are living animals that, for whatever reason, are existing and breeding in suitable unpopulated areas, exotic pets that have either been abandoned or have escaped.

This animal, however, is only seen at dusk moving swiftly through the marshy grasses near the River Trent. It simply appears from nowhere then after a few seconds it vanishes into nothing.

Georges Hill

A peculiar and unsavoury spectre is said to haunt the leafy Georges Hill near the village of Calverton. Sometimes it is just perceived as a hazy black mist gliding amongst the shadows and on rare occasions will form into a menacing apparition.

During the day the dense woods form a dark tunnel over this quiet lane, at night, the brightest moon would barely penetrate the winter bareness, in summer it would be almost pitch black. It was on such a night that Lawrence Bardhill was trudging up the hill. He had been to the Nottingham Goose Fair and as he had spent all his money on the sideshows he had to walk home. As he heard the village church clock strike midnight he became aware of something by a gateway. As he passed by he made out someone standing by the front of the gateway. Lawrence felt intimidated by the silent figure. It had a wide-brimmed hat not unlike the Puritan style and no features were visible. The rest of his dress was dark but Lawrence noticed quite a large silver or gold chain around its neck. Feeling totally threatened by whoever or whatever it was, Mr Bardhill moved over to the other side of the road and hastened his pace.

To his dismay, the figure moved away from the gateway and began to follow Mr Bardhill. He began to walk even faster, almost jogging: glancing back he saw the silent black shape a few yards behind, it seemed to be gliding in a fluid-like manner and quite rapidly. Lawrence was then totally terrified and began to run. For several hundred yards the figure stayed behind then suddenly drifted into another gateway. Quite relieved, but wary, Lawrence ran like hell until he was home.

He was so badly traumatized that he spent the night on the settee with the lights on. His brother-in-law visited next morning and was astonished to see Lawrence looking so drawn. He was also shaking as he described the events to his bemused relative. It was a week or more until Lawrence was completely over the trauma.

In 1977, a villager was passing under the leafy canopy when he observed a weird swirling black mass in the middle of the road. Was it a cloud of midges? No, as he got a few yards away the strange mass just evaporated leaving an air of pure evil in its wake. There were two reported encounters in the 1980s: in the first, the figure was seen by a couple in a car passing through the dark glade late one evening. The sinister figure in black was illuminated in the car headlights then glided out of view. The couple, although curious, felt compelled not to stop and leave the safety of the vehicle.

A solitary lady motorist was passing through the wooded hill late one night. Suddenly, she felt odd; she glanced in the rear view mirror and was horrified to discover she had an uninvited passenger on the back seat. All she could make out of the shadow-like thing was that it had a wide-brimmed hat. The thing vanished on the brow of the hill. The traumatized lady then sped off well above the speed limit and almost collided with another vehicle in her haste to get away from the place.

Sarah Meakin of Carlton was leaving a house in Calverton after babysitting on a warm summer night. She was driving up Georges Hill when she noticed the air temperature drop to almost freezing cold. Then the sensation of something pushing her seat forward. She looked in the mirror and saw a black shape with no face. She looked ahead and then glanced back but the thing had gone and it was warm again.

Above: *The Goose Fair, a popular local event.*

Right: *Georges Hill; at night a dark spectre may follow the unwary traveller.*

This apparition seems to show all the characteristics of what spiritualists describe as an 'Elemental', a morbid entity that was never created from the mind of any one living person, psychic residue fused into a black human shape with little to distinguish it; only the silver or gold chain may offer an idea as to part of the identity. These fusions form into a menacing, ice-cold apparition. It is claimed that such entities can be 'created' by witchcraft, séances or 'Ouija' sessions. It is a brave or foolhardy person who walks Georges Hill after nightfall!

Unicorn Hotel, Gunthorpe

The Unicorn Hotel has a room that is supposedly haunted by a vague wraith thought to be the ghost of a small child who came to grief here. One former assistant manager, Tom, reflected on a curious incident of a few years before. Two Canadian ladies, sisters, arrived quite late one evening to ask if there were any rooms vacant but not room X. Bewildered, Tom asked them why. Apparently fifteen years ago they had shared this particular room. In the middle of the night one of the girls, (as they then were) had awoken to see her sister standing at the foot of her bed. She asked her what she was doing and the answer came from the adjoining bed, 'I'm not out of my bed'. She was adamant she was not dreaming and that someone had been at the end of the bed. A colleague told Tom of an incident. He observed a dishevelled man enter the hotel early one morning. It later transpired that the man had checked in the previous evening and was given room X. In the middle of the night his bedclothes were suddenly pulled away in a violent manner twice so he spent the rest of the night in his car rather than endure the experience a third time.

SIX

EAST OF NOTTINGHAM

Newark Castle

Newark Castle stands majestically on the sloping banks of the River Trent. There has been a castle on this site since 1068. This structure would have been built by the Normans. Much of the building in existence today was built by Alexander the Magnificent; he was the lord of the manor of Newark, and the Bishop of Lincoln in the early twelfth century. He designed the three-storey gatehouse which now has stood the test of time and remains the only Romanesque structure of its type in Great Britain. Alexander also built the angled south-west tower was known locally as, 'King John's Tower'. It is uncertain if the king resided in the tower but he did die within the fortification in 1216.

Improvement work was undertaken in the fourteenth century. The curtain wall was rebuilt and two elaborate towers were added. The tower in the centre of the hall was designed as a keep. Further work undertaken a century later introduced fireplaces and window glass. In 1560, Newark Castle was leased to Sir Francis Leeke and in 1581 to the Earl of Rutland. After the Earl's death the castle was passed on to his son-in-law, Lord Burghley. He made many improvements and introduced so many comforts that the place became popular with royalty.

During the Civil War, Newark Castle held out for the Royalist cause and the castle was garrisoned by Royalist troops until ordered to surrender by the king. After the surrender, orders were put out to demolish all siege works, including Newark Castle. The place became a hovel with squatters and looters taking away timber, stone and other materials. The ruined castle remained in possession of the Crown from 1547 and in 1848 it became the first monument to be restored at government cost.

In the late 1800s the grounds were landscaped and work was undertaken to conserve the ruins with the wall tops capped with concrete. The north-west tower was also given a new roof. It is now a symbol of the town, a popular place to sit at lunchtimes amidst pleasant surroundings and perhaps see an open-air concert. The tourist information centre is based here and at night the castle is floodlit, creating an enigmatic scene. But there may be a darker side.

There is an unseen but tangible presence that periodically forms. Also peculiar noises and electrical problems have left staff baffled. One of the rangers claims to have in some way been

Newark Castle, a typical haunted old pile. Kings and queens may still roam these ancient ruins.

Another view of the proud fortification.

'influenced by something', almost taken over in a similar fashion to a spiritual medium taking on the personality of a discarnate entity.

Apparently in the early 1990s a party of ghost hunters descended on the place in order to see once and for all if there was indeed evidence of a ghost or ghosts. Thermometers were placed about to test for drops in temperature and a video camera was kept handy. Tape recorders were left running in unoccupied areas. They did, by all accounts, not just hear and experience unnatural goings-on but were so scared by one incident that they fled the place; they were not forthcoming with what had caused this reaction. Speaking from experience, ghost hunters are fairly hardened characters and not easily spooked: it would have to be something highly malevolent to drive out a team of experienced ghost hunters.

There is speculation that the ghost or ghosts may be of King John, Oliver Cromwell or any of the other kings and queens who have undoubtedly resided here. Of course it could be anyone. A Saxon burial ground was discovered and disturbed. Although rare, it is believed that Saxon ghosts still manifest today. The daytime visitor should have no such problems as it seems the most popular time for strange things to happen is the ungodly hour of 4 a.m.

Balderton Hall

Balderton Hall in Newark was built in 1840 for a wealthy banker by the name of Thomas Godfrey. The Godfreys resided there for forty years before a succession of well-off families. It later became part of a hospital and in 1942 served as accommodation for various detachments of

Balderton Hall in the 1920s.

the American military. Increasing numbers of American airmen were based at many of the RAF airfields around Newark and many personnel would stay wherever was available.

This might explain the mysterious airman who periodically appears in the grounds. He is a young chap, very tall, who moves about quite swiftly. He has a uniform of the USAAF, (United States Army Air Force) and on one shoulder of his smart tunic is the insignia of a blue circle with gold wings on a number eight, the eighth Air Force, the largest group to carry out bombing missions over Europe.

In 1993 the threat of demolition hung over Balderton Hall. The hospital closed and stood empty for several years then the grounds were sold to a property developer for a large housing estate. Many other buildings were gone but thankfully the hall will remain; it is now an office complex. Two unknown apparitions in similar styles of dress sometimes slowly glide through the main hall. They appear from their clothing to be late Victorian or early Edwardian. They are both of advancing years with long, blue, high-necked dresses. A cheerful phantom may be encountered on one of the top floor corridors, a young girl from the Victorian era running silently up and down the passage with a contented smile. Apparently she only lasts for a few seconds before vanishing.

Newark Friary

Phantom monks are quite common to those who see ghosts. A medium once said to me, 'Monks are two a penny'. I have never seen a full-blown apparition and would indeed like to do so – a monk would be fine. Perhaps the dissolution and terrible persecutions have created so many ghostly monks?

Newark Friary was founded in 1507 by order of King Henry VII. He was very fond of the place and on his death left £200 to the friary; this was a massive fortune at that time. This enabled the friary to grow and improve conditions for the monks. They were a common sight in the town and got on well with the townspeople. They wore grey tunics with wide sleeves of a coarse Hessian fabric; they had a high, pointed black hood with the traditional knotted rope for a girdle. They still had to beg and relied on donations, two rather generous being from John Barton from nearby Holme and a Mr Robert Brown, who bequeathed the friary 'fourpence a week and a fedder bed'.

Friary is not a common word for such places, monastery or priory being the usual. I recall asking for directions on a case somewhere, 'Can you tell me where the friary is?' 'Just in the village opposite the pub'. Puzzled, we found it, a fish and chip shop! When Henry VIII came to the throne the fear of impending trouble soon affected all religious orders. One of the friars at Newark, Father John Forest, stood up to the king's policies and was burnt at the stake in Smithfield after a short incarceration in the Tower of London. Many other monks died terrible deaths as the Dissolution took hold.

The friary closed in 1534. By 1539 all the surviving friars had left Newark. The ruined building was left to the elements. The remains were demolished in the seventeenth century, although an intact portion was developed into a private residence by Sir Francis Leake. Over the years rumours of phantom monks became quite common. This idea was strengthened when several skeletons were discovered in 1976. Archaeologists established the bones as medieval. The skeletons showed the terrible injuries inflicted on the unfortunates, most likely former friars.

The friars' graveyard has now been built on, which has led to other suggestions of haunting phenomena. Two building contractors on separate occasions claimed to have seen a shady, hooded figure emerge through a wall and vanish in the old cellars that was adjacent to the graveyard. Further work in 1987 unearthed yet more evidence: some thirty skeletons were found during excavations. This act might have stirred up psychic unrest as one of the contractors was disturbed to observe a hazy, black monk hovering just off the ground in front of him. Periodic sightings of dark hooded figures continue, and probably will for centuries.

Southwell

It is difficult to know whether to describe Southwell as a large village or a small town. Opposite the minster is the rambling Saracen's Head Inn. Among the several ghosts reputed to walk here is a former king, no less. King Charles I is said to have sought sanctuary here after the Civil War when his own Parliament were after him and the Roundheads also wishing to slay him. On the night of 4 May 1646 he was captured. He was later executed.

In 1651 the inn, which at that time was called The King's Arms, had a new host who decided to change the inn's name due to his hatred of the Royalist policies. It became The Saracen's Head Inn. This was thought to be an insult to the Royalists as a Saracen sword was used to behead King Charles I. The name change must have stirred unrest as the clearly recognizable king has been spotted in a room named after him, the King Charles Suite.

A dandy from the Regency period minces throughout the entire building as if he owns it. He is said to be quite tall but his powdered wig stands half a foot above his head. He allegedly emanates a sense of panic but is of a good nature if somewhat scatty.

Many hostelries have an article which is best left undisturbed. The artefact will be on display and earn a reputation as a thing of evil. In Market Harborough there is a portrait in the Three Swans Hotel. The unflattering portrait of the former host, John Fothergill, is never to be moved. It has been moved on rare occasions, such as refurbishment: glasses fly off shelves, an icy wind and a malevolent atmosphere builds up until the picture is returned.

Here there is a piece of willow pattern crockery known as 'The Plate of Evil'. In 2001 new owners soon decided to spruce the place up. They were told of the cursed plate but scoffed at such piffle. Soon the workmen arrived but none would move the dreaded plate. One of the owners pulled the thing off its bracket and threw it away: within a few months the owners were almost bankrupt and sold up.

A lady from the Victorian era haunts a toilet! At one time it was part of a bedroom in which the ghost, who maintains a cheerful demeanour, appeared regularly. Most recently, young Brenda Mellors attended a wedding reception here. She and several others had taken rooms. At nearly midnight she was jolted awake by loud cannon and gunfire. In obvious terror she got up and consulted her friend in the room next door but she had heard nothing. When the night porter was called for he admitted to hearing nothing either.

Besthorpe

Sand Lane, on the eastern tip of this quaint village, appears much like any other quiet country route. Where it takes a sharp turn there used to be a windmill. The old miller, Charlie, was something of a loner, bad tempered, a man of mystery who would just about pass the time of day, he did not welcome idle chat.

After a noticeable absence of Charlie, and the fact that the usually active sails on the mill had been roped down, someone decided to see if he was alright. Charlie was discovered dead on the kitchen floor: he had hacked his own throat with a carving knife. Several years after there were villagers claiming to have seen old Charlie moving mournfully about the now derelict windmill and the small yard. Eventually the old mill was pulled down but Charlie still lingers and frequently appears on the turn of Sand Lane where the windmill used to stand.

Holme

Another churchyard said to be haunted is that of St Giles in the tiny village of Holme. The psychic residue is believed to have come about after the morbid events of the year 1666. The Black Death took hold in many places, and Holme was one of them. As the rapid and particularly nasty symptoms caused many deaths, the churchyard gravedigger was busy indeed.

One woman called Nan Scott decided to take evasive action. She prepared a bag of warm skins and woollens, and also plenty of supplies, and one night crept into the church and made her way up to the belfry where she remained. Apart from the deafening mourning bells which were almost constant during the day, she felt safe from the living hell in the village. After what seemed like an eternity she noticed the bells had stopped and there seemed to be a doleful silence. She had not eaten for days and decided to see what was happening. She found that she was the only person left in Holme. Almost everyone had succumbed to the disease or had fled. She found some stale bread and hopefully uncontaminated water and returned to the silent and empty church. Eventually she died in her makeshift home, her skeleton discovered many months later.

Several years on normality returned and the plague became a distant memory. A scared-looking little woman would be seen nervously leaving the church then vanishing, also sounds of footsteps up in the empty belfry. Nan Scott is still seen today in the churchyard; she is to be pitied.

SEVEN

NEWSTEAD ABBEY

'Near this spot
Are deposited the remains of one,
Who possessed Beauty
Without Vanity
Strength without Insolence
Courage without Ferocity
And all the Virtues of Man
Without his Vices
This Praise which would be unmeaning flattery
If inscribed over Human Ashes
Is but a just tribute to the memory of
'Boatswain', a Dog
Who was born at Newfoundland
May 1803
And died at Newstead Abbey
Nov 18 1808'

So says the tribute, 'Epitaph to a dog', on a large memorial stone in the rambling grounds of Newstead Abbey. Boatswain (Bosun) was the beloved Newfoundland dog of poet and author Lord Byron. Boatswain died of rabies at only five years old.

Byron had expressed a wish to be buried with Boatswain but was interred in the little churchyard of St Mary Magdalene in Hucknall shortly after his death on 19 April 1824. Lord Byron was born on 22 January 1788. When his mother-in-law died it was expressed in the will that he change his last name to Noel in order to benefit and inherit half of her huge estate. He then signed himself 'Noel Byron' and boasted of having the same initials as one of his heroes, Napoleon Bonaparte. He was something of a character with an eye for the ladies. It is said he had sex with nearly 250 women in Venice in just twelve months. He is alleged to have had a romantic liaison with Mary Shelley, who became famous for her story of an obsessed doctor of medicine who believed he could restore life to the dead, *Frankenstein*.

Newstead Abbey: so much drama has left an indelible psychic mark on this unique ruin.

The pleasant grounds of the abbey where a 'White Lady' is said to walk.

Lord Byron, who encountered one of the ghosts at Newstead.

It is not the spiritual essence of Byron who haunts Newstead Abbey but his dog, Boatswain. He has been glimpsed on many occasions, often at dusk, bounding about near the monument. There are other ghosts at Newstead Abbey. It is claimed that Lord Byron himself experienced two happenings. A particularly unsavoury entity is known as 'The Goblin Monk', and a poem was written by Byron after his encounter with it:

> But lo! A monk, arrayed
> In cowl and beads, and dusky garb, appeared
> Now in the moonlight, and now lapsed in shade,
> With steps that trod as heavy, yet unheard;
> His garments only a slight murmur made;
> He moved as shadowy as the Sisters Weird,
> But slowly; and as he passed Juan by,
> Glanced, without pausing, on him a bright eye.

This verse featured in Lord Byron's most famous works, *Don Juan*, which remained uncompleted upon his untimely demise.

He spent most of his time at Newstead. The abbey was founded by King Henry. But King Henry VIII made himself the new owner of the monasteries and closed them all down. The abbot had cursed anyone who would attack the monasteries and this is thought to be how the goblin monk came about. It was an omen of death and brought misfortune to those it pestered. This included Byron, who was forced to sell the ruins to an old friend, Thomas Wildman, for £100,000.

In 1823 a young lady enquired about the possibility of renting one of the cottages on the estate. Her name was Sophia Hyatt, and as she appeared quite wealthy it was arranged for her to view one of the small dwellings, which she seemed satisfied with. She always wore a white dress and become dubbed, 'The White Lady'. Mr Wildman allowed her full access to the estate and she was most content to wander the gardens.

She copied the inscription from Byron's tablet:

> But 'tis past, and now for ever
> Fancy's vision bliss is o'er;
> But to forget thee, Newstead – never,
> Though I shall haunt thy shades no more

Then strangely, she removed her white bonnet, wiped the neck–tie ribbon against his vault then cut it away and wrapped it in paper.

Perhaps she beheld the goblin monk as she was run over by a carriage in Maypole Inn Yard in Nottingham on 28 September 1825: as a result of her terrible injuries, she perished. However, she would return. Thomas Wildman scoffed at the stories from the gardeners of a 'ghost' wandering about. An ex-military man, he had no time for such rubbish. Even so, the White Lady is still seen on rare occasions reliving her perambulations in the grounds.

One other ghostly effect is a column of greyish mist that forms in one of the panelled bedrooms. It is truly impossible to wander these ruins and grounds without absorbing the quite tangible essences of the characters that have lived and died here.

EIGHT

ANONYMOUS HAUNTINGS

BY LOUISE MARRIOTT

The Lace Market area is the oldest area of Nottingham, and was settled by the family of Snott long before the Norman Conquest. It was also the area that saw the most industrial changes as Nottingham embraced the industrial revolution and the vast demand for Nottingham lace. So there are many old buildings that have gone through several uses over the centuries. Tucked away up one of the streets is a former Methodist church, converted for other uses at the end of the Second World War.

No longer in use, staff many years ago reported seeing there a tall, thin figure that always appeared on one side of the building only. One person had a prolonged sighting when it appeared in the area she worked in, at the very top of the building. She followed it through several storerooms until it disappeared in front of her through a wall. Another sighting came when a visitor was using a vertical wall ladder that provided quicker access to the front area from rooms above. As they got to the bottom rung they turned to make their way across the hallway and saw what they later described as a tall young male in an over-sized demob suit walk in through the door they were intending to use and straight on. The visitor thought nothing of it, as they'd heard there were toilets in the front of the building, and carried along across the hall as intended. It was only when they reached the spot where they'd seen the figure that they realised it had walked through a solid wall.

One especially interesting sighting took place on the outside of the building. I spoke to a former staff member and I relate his sighting here:

'The building has a small passageway running up the right-hand side closed off by two locked iron gates. Someone asked me to go outside to the front of the building to unlock them, so that he could come in after moving his car. As I walked up to the first gate I glanced down the passageway and saw a figure walking down it towards me. I looked down to unlock the gate, looked back up again and the figure had disappeared. The figure was about 5ft 8in. in height and dressed in a dark ill-fitting suit and this description unfortunately matched that of the person I was opening the gates for. Thinking he had found a set of keys himself I went back into the building to carry on my work only to find him still inside, not quite ready to leave yet. I then realised the figure I had seen had walked straight through the first locked gate and was coming towards the second gate as I tried to unlock it.'

The laneways around the castle are now a flourishing, cosmopolitan area of private hotels, modern luxury apartment blocks and the bars and restaurants that shoot up to service the young professionals who live here. This is in mean contrast to what this area was like in days of yore. The laneways of the mid-eighteenth century would have been unrecognisable to today's tourist with their dark, sordid alleyways leading off from the castle and down to the Market Square. And it is to the story of one poor girl who lived here that we now turn.

Castlegate is better known for the famous haunting of Newdigate House, but one of the other buildings here holds a far darker, sadder story. I ask you to imagine the life of one of the many young girls of Nottingham that, through circumstances of birth, could not find a position as a servant in one of the many grand merchant houses. The girl we are focusing on earned her living as a prostitute working in a brothel, just yards away from the castle entrance. The building she worked from has been closed for some years now, but in my early childhood was open to the public. I still recall visits there with my mother, and the feeling of unease I felt (even then) when we climbed the staircase and passed a doorway blocked by a large display cabinet full of dolls. To many people dolls, with their impassive stares, are unsettling. And the contents of this cabinet positioned in front of the door are still vivid to me nearly forty years later. The dolls were large wooden and ceramic Victorian manikins with dead eyes, dressed in handmade linen dresses and sailor suits. But the cabinet masked a room with a dreadful history.

With the room's position at the top of the building, and towards the back, it was ideal for use as an office for the administrative staff and it was duly decorated and all the paraphernalia for the organisation of the museum moved in. But rumours have surfaced that the staff found it impossible to work in there. The room was always icy cold and the cries of a baby were heard coming from the walls. Eventually the room was abandoned and the door blocked off and whatever haunts it left in peace. Mid-eighteenth century knowledge about the facts of life was rudimentary to say the least. A working girl who found herself pregnant either had to deliver a live baby or be able to conceal the birth of a stillborn within the brothel. She faced the gallows if found trying to bury a dead child. And so, the poor girl of this story found herself in a room at the back of the house giving birth and she delivered a stillborn infant. This dead babe was then bricked up in the wall.

The discerning traveller wanting to stay in Nottingham will find private hotels guaranteed to give an exceptional standard of service whilst being situated far away from the bustling streets of the centre of the city and its nightlife. It is to one of these that we turn now.

At their request we will not identify the building concerned but feel our reader will enjoy hearing about another previously unheard of haunting in Nottingham. The building is very old with a warren of corridors, rooms and cellars (and the obligatory caves beneath, so familiar to any property in the city known as the Queen of the Midlands). Our first story comes from a time when my partner and I stayed in the hotel to see the New Year in. Owing to my partner's work we had to book at the last minute and found the place on the word of a friend in Nottingham who knew the hotel to have a very good reputation.

As it turned out, we were the only people staying over that period as the hotel had recently changed hands and the new owners hadn't managed to get advertising out in time for the Christmas/New Year period. We both looked forward to a quiet time with all of the city's attractions just a short walk away. We were given a room at the very top of the building, and because we knew ourselves to be alone we decided to take advantage of the communal bathroom in the corridor outside the room so we could both take showers at the same time.

The haunted Sir John Borlaise Warren, a popular town pub.

Apart from little food parcels left outside our door every night by the management we remained undisturbed. Except, that is, for the sound of the doors on our floor being opened and slammed shut every time my partner went outside to use the other shower.

At first I assumed someone else had booked in, but eventually we realised there was a pattern to the disturbance and that we were indeed alone. Neither of us dared to take a look into the corridor as the sound of doors slamming reverberated around the walls. The new management have since reported the apparition of a young serving girl in one of the top rooms, and the very solid apparition of a gentleman who stands at the bar as if waiting to be served, only to fade out of sight once approached.

Canning Circus (west)

Canning Circus started life as a muddy area of intersecting tracks above Chapel Bar, the main entrance into the old city of Nottingham. As with most large conjunctions of trackways outside city walls, the area was the final resting place for those poor souls not allowed burial in consecrated ground. Suicides and felons hung on the gallows found themselves laid here in the superstitious hope that their sprits would be confused by all the routes available to them and not be able to find their way back to haunt those they might blame for their predicament.

The Circus today is still a busy junction of roads leading out of Nottingham and is framed by buildings all with their own rumours of ghostly activity. UK Paranormal have taken an especial interest in the area and I would like to share with you here some of their findings. It wasn't until the Municipal Reform and the Enclosure Awards of 1835-1865 that land on the outskirts of the old city was made available for development, so much of this area lay undeveloped until then. However, it is recorded that in 1796 a large wooden stile on the crossroads was replaced by what is now the Sir John Borlase Warren public house.

The history of the building beyond this is unknown, but it would seem that it was built as a private house, and was converted to a coaching inn in 1814. In layout it still resembles a residence, with a warren of rooms and stairways laid out over three floors. The servant's rooms still exist, unchanged, in the roof. However, it was the area below the private flat that was catching attention. UK Paranormal investigated the building in 2005 and found staff talking of sometimes violent poltergeist activity in the private flat and a generally unsettling atmosphere that comes and goes in its vicinity.

Their investigations, however, were limited to the caves beneath the building due to a private party being held in the bar. This situation was to lead to one of the best audio recordings captured by the team to date. EVP stands for Electronic Voice Phenomenon, and is an area of paranormal investigation that is fast gaining attention. UK Paranormal always make use of sound recorders in their work in the hopes of catching something that was not apparent to the human ear at the time. Looking back at this particular investigation they were very glad they didn't hear what was to come to light!

The caves below the Sir John Borlase Warren extend another three storeys under the building and spread out into a series of long alleyways connected by a single passageway running through their middle. It was in the left-hand branch of the furthest cave that the team settled themselves. As is habitual, a Dictaphone was left recording in the connecting corridor (as much to catch the sound of anyone who might try to sneak up on the team as for any other reason) as the team made ready the first of many experiments. All team members were approximately twelve yards away from the corridor and the Dictaphone.

Keeping their spirits up with banter, so to speak, one of them joked that the spooks would be too busy rummaging through their personal belongs (left many feet above them in the bar) to make an appearance that night. Later review of the tape caught more then they expected when a rough male voice is heard to answer "There is plenty of that!"

Tequila's Restaurant

Anyone who visited Tequila's in its time might have noticed the high vaulted ceilings, the beautiful brickwork and its resemblance to stabling. This may be due to the early history of the block of buildings that make up the edge of the Circus. They date back to the 1850s when they were used as a livery stables, and then as a home for monument masons and a funeral home run by the Palethorpe family. The building were again used for this purpose by the Co-operative Funeral Services and later, Lymms' funeral directors. At one stage the mortuary became a fish and chip restaurant. The buildings, at this time, are Tequila's Mexican restaurant and a bar.

The team visited the building after hearing that the manager was experiencing an unsettling feeling in his office on the second floor, so unsettling in fact that they found the poor man had moved himself (and the small amount of equipment he needed to conduct his business from

A view of Tequila's Restaurant.

Ben Bowers Restaurant. Nottingham's longest-running haunting?

day to day) to a small billet next to the kitchen. Unfortunately nothing was found to suggest an active haunting was underway, just as importantly no evidence of deception was found: a stalemate situation, ghosts remain aloof when hunted!

Ben Bowers

The building housing Ben Bowers Restaurant stands at the pinnacle of Derby Road. Courting couples would meet under the elegant clock before making their way down into the city for an evening of entertainment. The building is said to have been a coaching inn, and Ben Bowers himself was a local tramp who made some small living odd-jobbing. I am not sure whether he still haunts the building, but haunted the building certainly is.

Owner and manager Tony established his renowned restaurant here thirty years ago and his first experience came early on as the staff relaxed at the end of a busy night. At this time the main room was split into two with a dividing wall running across the room. It was approximately 2 a.m. in the morning and they were all celebrating a successful day's work in their fledgling business when the figure of a woman in a shawl was seen to glide along the dividing wall.

She has been seen many times since, especially in the back portion of the building that now houses the kitchen. Parts of the building show signs of fire and one visitor described walking in and sensing the top room being full of smoke. At one time the building was a drugstore and when Tony was renovating he found the huge mortars used for mixing compounds still *in situ* in the cellars below. It is said that the chemist set fire to the cellar many years ago before making his way to the top of the building and throwing himself from an upstairs window. Echoes of this sad affair seemed to linger in the upper rooms, where staff told Tony they felt uneasy but, as is often the case in these instances, a small prayer was said in the area, and the spirit was told there was more to the afterlife then endlessly roaming the sight of their demise. This seemed to work as the atmosphere cleared.

Is it the mournful shade of Ben Bowers that periodically appears in the building?

And finally, a view of the Victorian cellars which lie underneath the Broadmarsh Shopping Centre. What lurks within them, waiting to be discovered?

Other local titles published by Tempus

Haunted Birmingham

ARTHUR SMITH AND RACHEL BANNISTER

From the landlady who haunts the site of her death, the two workmen who died during the building of the Town Hall, the late Mayor who still watches over the city, the last man to be publicly hanged in Birmingham, and many more ghostly goings-on, *Haunted Birmingham* will delight all those with an interest in the supernatural history of the city.

0 7524 4017 9

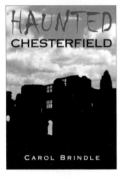

Haunted Chesterfield

CAROL BRINDLE

Journey through the darker side of Chesterfield, a town steeped in spooky tales that will captivate anyone with an interest in the supernatural history of the area. From creepy accounts of churches and shops to tales of hospitals, pubs and cinemas, Haunted Chesterfield contains a chilling range of ghostly phenomena. Drawing on historical and contemporary sources, you will hear about the ghost child of the Yorkshire Bank, the phantom footsteps which haunt the tower of St Mary and All Saints church, the ghost of George Stephenson at the Pomegranate Theatre, and many more ghostly goings-on.

0 7524 4081 0

Haunted Coventry

DAVID MCGRORY

Haunted Coventry features spooky stories galore from the city and surrounding area. From the Phantom Monk of Priory Row to ghostly grey ladies, a spectre that appears to do the washing up, a phantom lorry, spooky séances, and the Devil himself, rattling chains at Whitefriars – just a taste of the many restless spirits to be found in haunted Coventry – this fascinating collection of strange sightings and happenings in the city is sure to appeal to anyone intrigued by Coventry's haunted heritage.

0 7524 3708 9

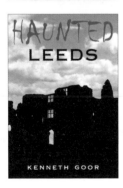

Haunted Leeds

KENNETH GOOR

Journey through the darker side of Leeds, a city steeped in spooky tales. From creepy accounts of the city centre and surrounding suburbs to phantoms of the theatre, haunted hotels and pubs, an ex-librarian who haunts Leeds Library, the ghost of a murderer at the Town Hall, Mary Bateman the Leeds Witch, as well as many other spectral monks, soldiers and white ladies, Haunted Leeds contains a chilling range of ghostly goings-on.

0 7524 4016 0

If you are interested in purchasing other books published by Tempus, or in case you have difficulty finding any Tempus books in your local bookshop, you can also place orders directly through our website

www.tempus-publishing.com